All rights reserved.
Copyright © 2004 by Barbara Del Buono

Published by:
The Ellingsworth Press, LLC
680 Main Street
Watertown, CT 06795
Telephone 860 274 7151
Toll Free: 877-ELLPRES (355-7757)
E-mail: ELLPRESS@aol.com
Website: www.ellpress.com

No part of this book may be reproduced or transmitted in any form or by any means, electronic or mechanical, including photocopying, recording, or by any information storage and retrieval system, without permission in writing from the publisher, except in the case of brief quotations embodied in critical articles and reviews.

The paper used in this book meets the requirements of the American National Standard for Permanence of Paper for Printed Library Materials.

Del Buono, Barbara
"A Man" To Remember: The Inspiring Story of Saint Nick
– Sequel to Acknowledged A Man / Barbara Del Buono, 1st ed.
1. Inspiration   2 Victims of Crime   3 Brain Injury

1st ed.
p.cm.
Includes index.
ISBN: 0-9605698-7-1

First Edition
Manufactured in the United States of America

"A MAN" TO REMEMBER

The inspiring story of Saint Nick

Sequel to
ACKNOWLEDGED A MAN

by Barbara Del Buono

THE ELLINGSWORTH PRESS, LLC

Also by Barbara Del Buono

Jesse and Anna Webb
A Story and History of the
Webb Family in America

When Two Become One
The Miracle In Marriage
Co-Author with
Attorney John Del Buono

ACKNOWLEDGED A MAN
Survivor of Assault in the YMCA

Come Holy Spirit
A Guide to Confirmation
in the Roman Catholic Church

This book is dedicated to John Nicholas Del Buono and all the people who helped me write his inspirational story.

A special dedication is made to his devoted father, John, and his loving sister, Mary, both of whom worked so hard to make Nick's life as good as it could be.

Table of Contents

1. Acknowledged A Saint………..………..….1

2. Nick's Story…………………………….....14

3. Mary's Story, Loving Sister……………….26

4. Mary D'Agata , Friend and Nurse………..45

5. Kevin Trembley, Friend…………………..50

6. Gail St. Mary, Friend and Aide…………...56

7. Gail's Sons……………….………..….…...63

8. Carly Fenn, Friend and Aide…………..….68

9. Debra Vienneau, Friend and Aide……..….72

10. Nicole Del Buono, Devoted Niece…..…...78

11. Dr. Allen Chatt………………………....…81

12. Dr. Stephen Sarfaty…………………..…….84

13. Dr. Stephen Rubenstein…………………....90

14. Sandra Parsons, Private Investigator….….92

Table of Contents
(continued)

15. Paul Hultman, Artist..........................94

16. Ann Sheldon, School Teacher...............97

17. Deborah Del Buono, Sister..................98

18. Johnny Del Buono. Nephew...............101

19. Joan McKnight, Sister......................104

20. Cathy Jewett, Sister........................106

21. Sally Houseknecht, Sister..................108

22. Peter Casteel, Nephew......................113

23. Amy Dean, Niece............................118

24. Kyle Houseknecht, Nephew................121

25. Christina Greenway, Cousin...............124

26. Judie Gunn, Cousin.........................129

27. Ted Phipps, TBI Caregiver.................132

28. Jacqueline Daddona, Nurse................137

29. Death Cannot Vanquish Love.............139

1

Acknowledged A Saint

"A Man"

by Emily Dickinson

Fate slew him, but he did not drop;
She felled—he did not fall—
Impaled him on her fiercest stakes—
He neutralized them all.

She stung him, sapped his firm advance,
But, when her worst was done,
And he, unmoved, regarded her,
Acknowledged him a man.

John Nicholas Del Buono, our beloved son, Nick, epitomizes what Emily Dickinson described in her poem about what it means to be "A Man." No one expects the worst to happen in their life, but it sometimes does. And it did to Nick. How you handle the worst determines just how much a man you are.

Nick lived a normal life as a youngster and as a young man. But in his 25th year of life tragedy struck suddenly, swiftly, criminally, when a baseball bat wielded by an angry man struck our son's head and knocked him to the floor of a YMCA weight lifting room. He was beaten over and over, four or five times — all in the head, causing one of the most serious brain injuries one can endure and live. The life Nick had known flowed out of his body in a pool of blood on that YMCA floor. But the criminal who tried to kill him could not touch his immortal spirit.

It is his spirit that inspires this book. Out of this tragedy a saint was born, and those of us fortunate enough to have been by his side for the twenty-six years and three hundred twenty-seven days that he lived after having been injured, have a yearning to tell the world that ordinary saints do live and are on earth for us to know, to love, and to serve. They affect our lives and infect them with the greatest treasure on earth—the power to love and be loved in return. What a glorious quest we began when Saint Nicholas was born that tragic day!

Father Joseph Hallissey, another saint, was the chaplain at the University of Oklahoma in 1948-49 and 1950. Nick's father was a student in the law school at the university. Father Hallissey often sat on the back porch of his rectory and some of the students would come by to chat with the priest who was rumored to be "seven years younger than God." It was his age that impressed the young men and the wisdom he imparted on these wonderful evenings.

On one such evening Father Hallissey asked the young men, "If an Englishman gets on a boat and crosses the Atlantic Ocean and gets off in New York City, does he instantly become an American, or, is he still an Englishman?" Of course the young students responded, "He's still an Englishman!"

Nothing had changed in the man's life to make him an American just because he stepped on American soil. "Well," Father Hallissey said, "if you want to be a saint in Heaven when you die, what should you be on earth before you die?" The young men timidly responded, "You have to be a saint on earth."

This story was the eulogy that Nick's father gave at his Memorial Mass in celebration of Nick's life at the beautiful Immaculate Conception Church on the Green in Waterbury, Connecticut. His father concluded the eulogy by saying, "Our son Nick was a saint before he died. Our son Nick is now a saint in Heaven."

Nick's father wanted those in attendance to know that Nick was a saint on earth and that he had achieved this status in the hardest way possible. But if he could do it, with all of the limitations life put in his way, then any one of us can do it. Nick is proof that this is true. And it is also a warning. Heaven is not easily won and it is the dwelling place of saints and angels. You must become one before you can enter the gate.

For those of us who are blessed with the grace to believe in God, death is a reality that we think of all of our believing life. We realize that our short life on Earth is the testing ground for where our souls will go after we die. And that life will last for an *eternity*. Our goal is Heaven and such a goal is worth striving for!

As a result we are forever trying to become saints—often slipping and falling in the process, but always seeking to become one. Nick is that beautiful person who heeded the advice once given by a priest. "We're all called to be glorious saints. Don't miss the opportunity!"

What does it mean to be a saint? How do you become one? Someone once asked St. Thomas Aquinas how one could become a saint. His quick response was, "Will it." In order to "will it," each one of us must be absolutely convinced of God's love for mankind—and be willing to cultivate a humble heart.

Even if you are able to do all of this, not all of us can be a Mother Teresa, going out and gathering up the dying and the poor and the helpless from the streets of Calcutta. But then, there are always the dying, the poor and the helpless right in our own families and communities everyday of our lives.

A mother nurturing her helpless children can be a saint if she does it in accordance with the will of God. Likewise, a father working and giving all he has to his family can be a saint. Becoming a saint means trying to do God's will in everything we do, everyday, in the *kindest* way possible. It means loving those in our lives *no matter what their condition*. If we are able to do this, then we will have the support of God in all of our endeavors. This is what sainthood is all about. It is not an unattainable goal!

In our church, the Catholic Church, November 1st is celebrated as the feast day of All Saints. This special day is in the church calendar in order to honor the many saints who exist but who will never be canonized and made famous by their good works.

Nick's sainthood falls in this class. In order to know how he came to be a saint we must know something of his life. He achieved this distinction by enduring and *loving life* from the moment he was born. Nick was an extrovert, an outgoing, although shy person. He was interested in everything as a child—

"A Man" To Remember

and I do mean everything.

One memory comes to mind. One summer day, when Nick was about eight or nine years old, Nick's sister came running in the house to get me. She was so excited I couldn't understand her so I quickly followed her outside where she was tugging me to go. She guided me to a storm sewer in the street near our home where the grate covering it had been removed. Nick was down in the storm sewer and I excitedly asked him, "What in the world are you doing down there?" "I want to know where it goes," he replied. I quickly hauled him out of the sewer and we went home and had a discussion about storm sewers and their purpose in life.

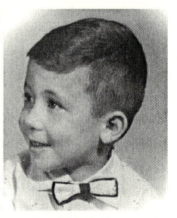

Nick was fun-loving, and a great tease—especially with his mother. In one of my early stages of vanity I bought a wig to wear when I was too busy (I thought) to do my hair in an attractive way. Nick thought that was the silliest thing I ever did. He hated that wig and teased me unmercifully about it. One day I came home from shopping and parked the car in the street outside our home and Nick was outside playing. He came over to where I was getting packages out of the car and ripped the wig right off of my head and handed it to me. I was totally mortified. Had the neighbors seen me? I have never worn a wig again in my life. He taught me a valuable lesson about what is important and it was that I should be myself and succeed on that basis or not at all.

Nick especially loved to accompany me on shopping trips even if it was only to the grocery store. On one occasion we were downtown looking for a parking place in front of the department store where we wanted to go. Another car was pulling out of a prime parking spot and I pulled in front of the departing car so that I could back into its space when it left. But as it pulled out another car behind it shot into the space too quickly for me to be able to back into the spot I had been waiting for. I was visibly upset with the driver of the sneaking car and glared at him. He noticed that I was still waiting and not moving and quite unhappy with what he had done. I yelled out the window at him, "You illegally took that space and you should be ashamed of yourself." He came over to my car window and said, "Well, what do you want me to do about it, leave?" I quickly said, "Yes, I do." To my amazement, he said, "Okay," and got in his car and pulled out leaving the space open for me.

Well, this episode just about blew Nick's mind. "I can't believe you did that, Mom," he said. "Well, Nick," I replied, "I was in the right and then he did the right thing back." It was a great lesson for Nick and he never forgot it as he mentioned it many times when he would be laughing and telling his friends how his mother stood up for her rights over nothing more important than a parking space.

Nick could be quite the little con-artist when he wanted something. On another occasion he was downtown with his brother and they wanted a cup of coffee and didn't have the money for one. Nick went into a restaurant and asked a waitress for a plastic baggie and she gave him one. He went outside and

"A Man" To Remember

raised his foot and swiped the dirt from between the heel of his shoe and the sole and put it in the baggie. He then found his mark and told the young man that this baggie full of dirt was from the "Woodstock" concert. He offered to sell it to him for a dollar and the kid bought it. Nick and his brother enjoyed that cup of coffee immensely as they regaled over the con that Nick had just pulled off.

Nick was a strong and eager young lad. He dazzled all the kids on our block when we gave him a pogo stick for his tenth birthday by learning to balance himself so well on it that he could jump up and down on that pogo stick all around the block we lived on without getting off of it one time. This was a distance of about six hundred yards! No one but Nick could achieve this feat. As a result we always buy a pogo stick for our grandchildren and for our great-grandchildren on their tenth birthday—in honor of Nick.

But Nick was also a serious person who had a great faith, even as a child. He was especially in awe of a woman with child. He touched his sister's stomach with loving tenderness as she carried our first grandchild. He literally danced with joy in our living room when the word came that the baby had arrived and was a healthy boy.

He hated the thought of abortion and sobbed when a good friend told him that he had paid for his girlfriend to have an abortion. He very much lamented the fact that his friend was deprived of the opportunity to be a father to the child he had conceived. He cut off his relationship with this friend after that. Nick sincerely believed that every conception was blessed by God and that every birth is the promise that God has not given up on the human race. He also believed the opposite: that every abortion is a statement that man has given up on God—and that Nick would never do.

Nick left our home to join the Air Force and became a Still Photographic Camera Specialist. I believed the Air Force knew just what to do with Nick. I thought they were very smart to give him a camera instead of a gun!

Sergeant Del Buono wrote home often and we  wrote back to him. On one occasion I sent him an apple pie I baked from the apples we gathered from the tree in our back yard. I knew he would remember the summers he and his brother and sisters peeled ripe apples relentlessly while I made apple pies for the freezer. When it arrived he said it was smashed but he and his buddies enjoyed it anyway.

Nick's humor came through when he addressed one of his envelopes to me: "Mrs. John A. Del Buono (in care of the God Zeus). The return address was "Sing Sing House of Correction, Up the River, JailBird, U.S.A." On the back of the envelope it said, "Mr. Phelps This envelope will self-destruct in 10 seconds. Good Luck."

I have discussed other incidents in Nick's youth in the book I wrote about his life after brain injury, *Acknowledged A Man*. His faith, his passion for life, his ability to love, were all there as a child and these attributes never left, even after his life changed so dramatically.

How did Nick's life change? Due to the serious brain-injury he sustained, Nick was blind. But that was just one of his deficits! Only by taking care of someone whose brain has been so badly damaged can one really appreciate the marvelous organ all of us carry about in our heads. Without it directing us to do so, we could not even open and close our eyes; we could not walk or talk; none of our senses would work; we could not listen to a symphony or a rock and roll band. We could not jog or run, or engage in any sport—we could not even think. We could not be educated and learn. Nick lost all of this and more. His life after injury was reduced to the lowest level one can imagine. Lying in a hospital or nursing home bed, alive and conscious, was about all he could do.

After slowly awakening from a more than seven month coma, Nick started the new life that inspired all of us so much. With diligent help from those who were willing to give him a part of their lives, Nick became aware of his surroundings; he showed us that he still had the ability to think; he still was the stubborn person who wanted to explore everything and did so—even from a wheel chair when he could not see where he was going.

Though he couldn't see, he could still hear, he could touch, he could taste and even smell. With just this much going for him life started anew. He learned a gestural language that no doctor ever believed he could remember and then used over one hundred fifty of those gestures to get his messages across to us who cared for him.

When we were able to have him come home to live, rehabilitation started in earnest. He overcame the hated feeding tube and started to eat regular meals. With this accomplishment he proved that he did not need the opening in his throat for some possible future intubation. With that closed, he could then inhale more air and started speech therapy. He learned to talk—albeit in a limited fashion. But he stuck with his coach and persisted in his desire to know how to convey messages to us orally. He learned to feed himself, with help for guidance because he was blind.

With the assistance of a long-leg brace, and many others to follow, he learned to walk again and even managed to climb stairs. He never missed a family gathering because of stairs. He lived his role in the family as uncle with the greatest of ease. Nieces and nephews loved their Uncle Nick and were enthralled with all the games they could play with him, i.e., as the blind man who could kick a gymnastic ball to them; and the uncle who would listen while they read their children's stories to him and then give them a hug afterward.

As all of this happened, those of us who cared for him, who helped him in the bathroom with showers and dressing, received his appreciation by word and deed. "I appreciate it," he would say and mean it. When something was especially nice, there would always be the open arm (he could only use the left) and a great big hug.

His relationship with God was indescribable but I shall try anyway. When a new aide was to be interviewed I always had to ask the forbidden question, "Do you have any problem with Nick being very religious?" It was necessary for they were going to have to read the Bible to him and listen to the Mass being said on *EWTN* and *Mother Angelica Live* and other religious programs. They were going to have to accompany him to Mass in a Catholic Church on the occasions when we were able to get him there.

Nick made up his own gesture for God and it was to raise his left hand as high as he could get it and point his fingers toward Heaven. There were times when he would hold that hand up so long it hurt to watch but he would not bring it down until he and God finished whatever it was they were doing. "God is working on me," he would say and it was useless to try to get him to do anything else while this was going on.

Nick used the metaphors of angels and devils to describe what brain injury meant to him. After he slowly awoke from coma, blind and restrained day and night in a bed or chair, he believed he was in hell and that sometimes devils came and did horrible things to him and that at other times angels came to minister to him with kindness and were there to take him to Heaven. It truly is a very apt description of what brain injury is like for the victim.

Through all of this darkness, this hell that he lived in, he saw God and believed in himself and told us always that he loved life. He counseled all of us with our problems and the advice was always good. Most often it would be, "Love God." After a while we became used to that phrase and realized that it was the best advice we ever got about anything. He said it in such a way that it wasn't "preachy" or overly sentimental. Yet he got his message across in a reassuring way. It was just Nick, a man giving us the best advice he could.

Sometimes family members would come in a room and not even notice Nick—not even say hello. I would often get offended at this attitude but not Nick. He seemed to understand their feelings and not hold it against them.

Family members who did not take care of Nick were unaware of his ability to reason and think. This was demonstrated one Christmas day when we were playing a trivia game and Nick was sitting around the table with us. The question was asked, "What do you helicopter to the bugaboos for?" A lot of laughing went on as no one knew the answer. Nick got excited and all of us could see it. He was trying to say something and it turned out to be "sk-sk-ski." When the card was turned over and that was the answer, a silence fell on the room that was deafening. All of a sudden, everyone sitting around the table knew that Nick was still with us, that he could think and get his message across to us. It made quite an impression. It was one of those moments in life you never forget.

In all the years after his injury I never knew Nick

to deliberately be unkind to anyone. That does not mean that he was a powder-puff of a guy. He could reprimand someone in the most emphatic, but kind way that I have ever known. When an adult was talking to one of the young boys in a brusque and degrading way, Nick just let it be known he had something to say and it was, "I don't like your attitude." That stopped the conversation. It was to the point, but kind. He said to all of us that it's okay to reprimand someone but it must be with a kind attitude.

Nick could not abide people complaining about their life. And who can blame him? He had far more to complain about than any of us! He would tell them, "Get over yourself," and not be shy when he said it. Nick didn't have a lot of breath to say several words in a sentence so he had to make his meaning known in just a few words. He did this beautifully.

As a mother, I had the greatest gift any mother could have. I had my son come to the breakfast room and refuse to sit down until I came to him and he gave me a big hug and said, "Mom, I want God to bless you and me and our life." On most of these mornings I had the pleasure of having Mary, our oldest daughter, standing by his side. She was there to take care of him. I am a most blessed mother.

During part of Nick's rehabilitation at home, he tried to learn to write again. It was somewhat successful and gave us the opportunity to really know what was on his mind about many things. It is also another indication of his sainthood that should be shared.

2

Nick's Story

Nick was injured on June 25, 1977. Three months later he was sent to a nursing home because there was no place for young brain-injury victims to go except to nursing homes.

Each time I went to the nursing home I worked with Nick to improve whatever skills I could learn that he had. This was not an easy task as the only way you could discover what he was able to do was to try out different things with him, both on a physical and mental level.

We frequently sat in the hallway next to the nurses' station and I would do exercises with Nick by asking him to use the one arm that he could move to indicate where certain parts of his body were located. For instance, "Nick, touch your ear," or "Nick, touch your mouth—touch your knee—touch your other knee." These were fun things we could do to pass the time and it gave us both a good feeling because he was aware that he was conveying to me that he could still think and I was learning more and more just how much this was true. He was getting the message to me, through these gestures—and there were many of them, that he was still with us and needed our help to come back as far as he could.

On one occasion when we were doing our exercises, a speech pathologist observed us and told me she thought Nick should have speech therapy. I was thrilled with the thought and she obtained the necessary permission from the doctor. She began her work with Nick and just thirteen months after he was injured, on July 27, 1978, she wrote me the following note:

Dear Mrs. Del Buono

Nick's progress in receptive language areas has been excellent! By 'receptive' I am referring to his greater awareness in general, and his understanding of increasingly complex verbal language. For example, today I started asking questions about music. He was able to give appropriate yes-no answers (via headshake) to <u>all</u> questions—even very subtle.

I started talking about Barry Manilow, one of my personal favorites. I asked Nick to stop me when I named a song which Barry Manilow made famous. I gave the following: 'My Way', 'People' and 'Mandy'. Nick shook his head 'no' to the 1st two, and shook his head 'yes' to the appropriate song 'Mandy.' I asked him if he would like me to record some of Manilow's music & he said 'yes' via headshake. I will be doing so next week.

He gave other appropriate answers to questions requiring quite a bit of integration, e.g., 'what did Mr. Clean wear for jewelry in the old commercials.' Nick lifted his hand to his ear to indicate 'earring.' Responses to subtle questions of this nature indicate a good deal of receptive language integration as well as contact with one's environment.

We also worked on verbal communication. I am trying to get Nick to move his oral structures

<u>voluntarily</u> & thereby change the vowel sound 'ah' to 'ee' — 'o' and 'ai' three changes in the shape of his lips. Very slight changes did occur today which I find encouraging. This is a <u>very</u> difficult task for him but we will be working thru reflexive oral movements, such as those used in eating, in order to obtain more voluntary control.

On August 1, 1978, she wrote me another note:

Dear Mrs. Del Buono,

While it was inarticulate, Nick said 'I don't know' on more than one occasion today in response to questions. What was actually heard was 3 distinct units of speech in succession with appropriate vowels but no consonants. As a check on how meaningfully he was using this, I instructed him to answer by nodding 'yes' to a question if that was the correct response, shake head 'no' or if you do not know the answer say 'I don't know.' Nine questions were given, e.g., 'Are you a man?' 'Am I a female?' 'Is it going to rain tomorrow?' <u>All</u> of Nick's responses were felt to be appropriate.

I honestly don't know how clear his responses may be, how many sounds he will be capable of making or how much speech may be functional to him. I am thrilled with what he is doing now and because of his performance of late I do expect further progress. The ultimate satisfaction for me at this point, is that what Nick is using, he is using, for the most part, appropriately & meaningfully.

His understanding is not perfect but it has improved tremendously, & his receptive abilities are becoming increasingly functional.

In order to understand just what a great

accomplishment this was, another speech pathologist told me years later that it takes thirty-six muscles to say the word "church." The part of Nick's brain that controls language muscles had been greatly damaged and he would never get all of them back. What he did get back though was the ability to get his messages across orally more than ninety percent of the time.

While all of this was a thrill to us who were working with Nick, can you imagine the predicament this young 26 year-old man found himself in? One day he was a vibrant young man working out in a health club to keep his body in good shape. Then he slowly awoke from a coma lying in a nursing home bed, blind, unable to communicate or help himself in any physical way. He had no idea how this had happened or what was wrong with him. What terrible visions must have come to his mind!

The strength it took for him to endure, to persist in finding a way to live the life he loved is beyond human imagination.

There was never a time when he faltered in his desire to live and to make a new life for himself. During all of these stressful times Nick was asked to do some of the most impossible of tasks. This blind man sat on a round gymnastic ball, placing his feet on the floor in the proper place until he could balance himself. He had a long-leg brace put on his right leg, which was horribly contracted, and sat on the floor with his back to the couch with his feet straight out. He held this position until he could not endure the pain any longer.

Nick put his arms around his father and hobbled on his one good leg along the floor and up and down stairs so that he could learn the walking pattern again.

He practiced speech therapy every day for years just to be able to pronounce consonants so that he could speak again. The "f" and "v" consonants were very hard for him to master and the day he did it we all danced and clapped at his great accomplishment.

There were times we failed to give Nick credit for what he could do. We thought his memory was so poor he could not possibly enjoy books again so we read short magazine articles thinking he would not be able to remember the story from a book from one day to the next. The first time his aide and devoted friend, Gail St. Mary, tried this he was able to recall the story the next day with just the minimum of explanation about what had happened in the story the day before. After that books became Nick's great friends again.

Of course, the brain-injured Nick was not as intellectual as he had been before injury. Nevertheless, we learned some interesting and amusing things about him as we did therapy games with him. One of these games was to give him a word and ask him to make a sentence using that word. It is almost astounding that Nick could do this, but he accomplished it with an ease we never imagined. Also, it was a good exercise for us to test whether we could understand what he was saying. We could!

Thin—I don't want to be thin, I want to be muscular.

No—No is the opposite of yes.

None—Santa ate all the cookies and left none for the reindeer.

Open—I have an open heart full of love.

Found—I found out that God is in my life.

Bottom—The bottom is the last place I want to go.

Short—I am short of money for the gift.

True—I like to be true all the time.

Top—I have a top hat.

Old—I am going to be old someday.

Take—I don't take in the devils, I adore God.

Stand—I stand up for myself.

Remember—I remember that Jesus Christ died on a cross for me.

Rich—I am rich in love and happiness.

He—He gave bread at the Last Supper.

Stop—I want to have God never stop working on my eyes.

South—I was born south of the Mason-Dixon Line.

Light—I like the light from the sun.

Cry—I cry when I am hurt.

Full—I like to be full of money and food.

Found—I would be happy if I found a million dollars.

Mother—My mother is a woman who is pretty.

Stop—I love life and want Heaven to bless me and never stop.

Push—I get mad when people push me too far.

Play—I can play the flute.

Poor—I know that I am not poor.

Last—I don't like to be last at anything.

Out—I don't like to take out the garbage.

Girls—I have 6 sisters who are all girls and I like the girls.

From—I am from my mother's womb.

Happy—I am happy all the time.

Laugh—I like to laugh with my friends.

Give—I give great bear hugs.

He—He is working on my life.

More—I want to have God work on my life more and more and more.

Take—I want to have God take my life to Heaven.

Subtract—I want to have God subtract all of the devils out of my life.

Add—When you add 2+2 you get 4.

After—After the hour of 2:00 comes 3:00.

Back—Back is the opposite of front.

Open—I am open to the love of God.

Dark—I don't like to be in the dark.

Far—I think you are pretty far out!

Father—I love my father.

Below—I don't like to go below the water.

Big—I have a big heart full of love.

Slow—I want to be slow as a turtle.

Sad—I don't enjoy being sad.

Black—Black is the color of a witch's hat.

Rich—I want to be rich and famous.

Man—I want to be a good man.

Pull—Please pull my sleeve down.

These sentences are in Nick's own words and show the depth of his understanding. Gail was Nick's coach in most of these endeavors and sometimes they would work for days on a poem in order to come up with just the right words. This is the one for Summer.

> S-weetly we're blessed with summer fruit.
> U-nder a shade tree I play the flute.
> M-arvelous sunshine on my face.
> M-iles of walking at my own pace.
> E-njoying a cookout with family and friends.
> R-ays of hope, it never ends.
>
> By Nick Del Buono
> Dictated to Gail St.Mary,
> June 2000

One of my favorites is their Thanksgiving poem. This one took at least a week of hard work and when it was finished we read it on Thanksgiving Day.

"A Man" To Remember

This is a story about Pilgrims
Who settled here one day.
They traveled on the Mayflower,
From many miles away.

This story is about Indians
Who lived on this great land.
They met up with the pilgrims
And lent a helping hand.

They made a feast of turkey,
And with bread of corn and rye,
Delicious stuffing, sweet potatoes
And desserts like pumpkin pie.

Together they all joined in prayer
To give their thanks and love,
For everything they hold so dear
Especially God above.

    Nick

Nick wrote a poem about Christmas that still evokes tears each and every time I read it. With the help and guidance of his aid, Carly, our blind son painstakingly printed his feelings about Christmas with his left hand using a paper guide and built-up pen. Of course, it is framed and cherished.

GIFTS

For you this Christmastime I wish
So many precious things,
Not only gifts in packages
Secured with tinsel strings.

But treasures that are richer far
Than any gold can buy—
A scarlet leaf from Autumn's hills,
A bit of starry sky.

Health and peace, loved ones to share
A hearth fire burning bright,
And in your heart the song that rang
Across the world that night.

       Love
       Nick

Susan (Nick's sister) and Nick
On a sleigh ride with Aboo

My favorite, though, is a letter Nick wrote to his father for Father's Day in 1994. Carly Fenn, another one of his aides, helped Nick with the built-up pen and the paper guide to write this one too. Nick always printed everything, except his name "Nick" because he could not write. It was difficult and tiresome for him to try. Printing came easier because he could rest his hand between letters.

This card Is Filled with LOVE And it's all for you DAD

This is for you Dad, for the father I LOVE, for the one who cared all these years, but has never heard enough about how much I CARED.

So this is for you,

For the one who has helped me through, all my childhood fears and failures, and turned all that he could into successes and dreams. For the man who is a wonderful example, for what more men should be.

For the person whose devotion to his family, is marked by gentle strength and guidance and whose love of life, sense of direction and down to earth wisdom, make more sense to me now, than nearly any other thing I learned.

If you never knew how much I respected you, I want you to know it now, DAD, and if you never knew how much I admire you, let me just say that I think you're the best father that any kid ever had.

"A Man" To Remember

This card is filled with love for you Dad.

HAPPY FATHER'S DAY
GOD BLESS YOU
LOVE NICK

This letter is framed and hangs on the wall in his father's den.

Using the same method Nick composed a birthday card for me on March 1, 1986.

My Special Lady

Mom, I love you because you take time to take care of me with love and appreciation.

I like the way you take care of yourself.

You are a beautiful woman in body and soul.

I want you and me to love each other forever.

Thank you for being you.

I wish you a Happy Birthday.

    Greatfully,
    Nick

I was grateful he could still spell—even if he used the word "greatfully" instead of "gratefully." I will treasure this letter from him all the days of my life. I know what it took for him to be able to give it to me.

3

Mary's Story, His Loving Sister

The day that Nick was injured his sister Mary was in New York visiting her husband's parents and also attending the wedding of a friend. I had the unhappy task of calling her to let her and her husband, Tom, know of the terrible injury Nick had suffered. They flew home—by automobile.

Mary came to the hospital to see her brother and never left his side except to rest and take care of her family for the rest of Nick's life. The devotion she showed in caring for her brother is beyond words to describe. He loved his "Mary Ann" and she adored her brother.

Mary had two small children when Nick was injured but this did not deter her from having a huge influence in his recovery. She brought those children into Nick's life as naturally as she would have taken them to any sporting activity. We still treasure the many cards her daughter Amy wrote to Nick with flowers colored all over them.

Mary told me after Nick's death how thankful she is that his father saved his life by having him put on a respirator when the doctor had left orders that this was not be done. She is so right. We would never have had the opportunity to know the Nick that grew to be a middle-aged man had his father not done this.

As for me, I was blessed with an angel when our first-born, Mary Ann, was laid in my arms. We have shared life together ever since. She is my dearest friend. Nick was our first son and born just a year after Mary. They were close all of their lives and trusted each other more than anyone else other than Mary's husband.

Mary literally helped us raise her five younger sisters and two brothers. She and I used to share the pleasure of laying out all their clothes on the eve of Easter so that we would be on time for church the next morning. Patent leather shoes, lacy socks, frilly dresses and spring coats and bonnets were all placed in order by their beds so that we could help each child dress. Even her two brothers' clothes were all in place, including their hats for church. We had tremendous fun raising eight children and Mary was one of the reasons it was so good.

She is the most talented person I have ever known in being able to interpret the strengths and weaknesses of a child as she sits on the floor to play with them. She is now blessed with five grandchildren and they will never know until they are much older how blessed they are with the greatest grandmother any children ever had. I know that I have the greatest daughter any mother could ever wish for.

"A Man" To Remember

This is Mary's story about her brother:

Nick and I are the Oklahoma kids. It was the beginning of a lifelong bond. Our treks together began when Dad would take me and Nick and our sister Joan to Washington Park—climbing on the cannon and Dad pushing us so high on the swings that he could run under the swing and meet us on the other side. From that we learned how to swing high enough to jump over our play area fence into Grandma's garden. That was our first venture into trouble together.

Nick was baptized by Father Kenneth Fulton. He became a priest shortly after my parents were married, and has remained a lifelong friend and a tremendous influence in our lives. Father Fulton was also an avid baseball fan and would come from Oklahoma to Connecticut to visit and go to baseball games at Yankee Stadium. Father Fulton would amaze us with magic tricks and Nick became fascinated with them. He later became quite good with card tricks. When Father Fulton and the relatives from Oklahoma came to Connecticut, we would have wonderful trips to New York City to see the sites.

We moved to our home on Cronin Drive when I was in the second grade and Nick was in the first. We spent many years walking home from school together. Nick had a wide leg spread and it would take two of my steps to match one of his. We earned our mutual fear of dogs on one of these treks back to school after lunch. Thanks to Mom, the lunch time walk didn't last too long because she started the lunch program at school.

But the years walking home from school gave Nick and me the opportunity to become very close as kids. We talked about everyone and everything. We hated and loved the same teachers at Mt. Carmel School. That is where he met Sister Regina, who understood and appreciated Nick, and she became a lifelong influence in his life.

I was with Nick when he made his first Confession. I guess someone forgot to tell Nick he had to whisper in the confessional because the whole church heard his first confession. We made our Confirmation together too. Nick was picked to answer one of the Bishop's questions. Every spring there was a concert or show of some kind at Mt. Carmel School, and Nick was picked to be in two plays: the Story of Bernadette and Pinocchio.

Nick was cool, talented, curious and outspoken. He was a loner who got along well with others. He was my little brother, a fact I took advantage of every chance I got. But he was also my confidant and best friend.

One of the most curious things about him as a child was his relationship with the souls in purgatory and the Blessed Mother. When he prayed, he asked Mary to speak to Jesus for him. When he wanted something real bad, he would make a deal with the souls in purgatory to help him get it.

Murray Park was our neighborhood. The upper park is now a baseball field but when we were growing up it was a field of tall grass that made many adventures possible. We would play hide and seek in it and Nick's war games. At home we had four braided rugs in the "rumpus room" which would now be called a family room. Nick, Joan, Joe and I had our islands on these rugs and we would have every conceivable kind of adventure there. Each one of us had our favorite stuffed animals and Nick's was his chipmunk "Chippy."

Nick would never back down from a dare and I learned well from him. Nick built forts in the woods and took the challenge of climbing the water tower. In front of a bunch of our friends he dared me to rub poison ivy on my hands, knowing how allergic I am to it. Of course I took the dare and for a week suffered with the results. Nick and I both suffered Mom's wrath for our stupidity.

Nick received a pogo stick on his 10th birthday. He could jump longer than anyone in our street and many took the challenge. He graduated to stilts and could walk up and down the hill on them. During commercials on TV he would ride his bike to "Marcy's" market to pick up a snack and get home before the commercial was over.

Nick was one of the best baseball players in the neighborhood. When I played, Nick's team included me and Vinnie on one team and everyone else on the other. No one could get Nick or Vinnie out and I was the guaranteed out for this team. Once in a great while

"A Man" To Remember

I would actually surprise everyone.

For those old enough to remember, I was a Klicker and Nick was a Hood—with his Beatle boots safely hidden at Larry's house. Nick and I shared the discovery of Rock & Roll together—his favorites were the *Beach Boys,* the *Rascals* and the *Beatles'* Sgt. Pepper album. The *Moody Blues* became a family favorite group along with the saga of the *Lord of the Rings.* Nick's favorite TV shows were *Combat* and *Mission Impossible.*

Nick taught me how to play poker, 21, and Set Back at Murray Park. His card tricks fascinated many kids. Nick was great at ice-skating and pool. His nickname was "shark in the dark." Nick and I went to high school together and shared too many days cutting classes—with him playing pool and hanging out at the Handy Kitchen.

Joan and I shared with Nick his fear of calling a girl he liked for a date. Yet he dated wonderful girls. For such a cool dude, he was very nervous about calling girls for dates. Nick had a respect for girls that few guys had. He felt it was such an honor that girls could carry children and he demanded a certain level of self-respect from the girls he cared about. He had a friend who paid for his girlfriend's abortion and Nick would have nothing to do with him again.

Nick and I got our drivers' licenses a year apart. Nick would use the excuse that he had a date to have the car on the weekend even when he didn't. Mom and Dad bought a second car when Nick got his license. None of us will forget the time he got caught parking with the new car. We spent years of Friday nights at the Music Box and cruising downtown Waterbury.

"A Man" To Remember

Nick joined the Air Force in 1970 at the height of the Vietnam Conflict and that was the only time I ever had a fight with Nick. He was a photographer in the Air Force and spent most of his time in Colorado and California. Thank you Lord for answering my prayer and not sending my brother to Vietnam.

My most precious memory with Nick is when I was pregnant with my son Pete and how special he made me feel and how happy and excited he was at this child's birth and his becoming an uncle. But, after living in California, one winter back in Connecticut was all it took for him to return to California to study cinematography.

Nick came back home to work with me and Mom and Dad on a new publishing business enterprise: Ellingsworth Press, and its first published book – *When Two Become One*. He painstakingly produced and directed a TV commercial for the book—the memories of which are very precious to those of us involved in it.

Nick and I had a great time getting to know each other again. He did not return home with the same confidence he went into the Air Force with. He was now a man, searching for his life as a man.

Upon his return home, Nick's possessions included many books and his notebooks. One notebook cover in his handwriting stated, "Jesus is my brother.". During one of our parents' Christmas parties Nick got into a conversation about the Bible with one of Dad's lifelong friends. I was amazed at how much Nick knew of the Bible. I later learned that he had a close friend in

California who was a priest and they talked quite often about the Bible and the Catholic faith.

I had my family and some friends over to celebrate Tom's 29th birthday. Nick played horseshoes with our four-year old son Pete in the back yard. Pete was finally at an age Nick could enjoy. My beautiful little girl, Amy, who was only two, was fascinated with Nick from the day she met him and was around him every chance she got.

Nick got decked out to leave in his new car to meet a friend and hopefully meet some girls. He stopped combing his hair back and now parted it on the side as he was beginning to worry about his receding hairline. Tom and I talked with him in the driveway before he left. He was happy and looked great.

The next day, nine months after returning home from California, at age 25, Nick was assaulted at the YMCA by Joseph Tramontano, who is currently going on trial for another assault.

The rest of the story can be found in *Acknowledged A Man*, EXCEPT: I had the privilege of watching Nick grow into a man who became the person I admire most in this world and look forward to seeing at his mansion in the next life.

I prayed like I have never prayed before, or since, for Nick to come out of coma—and he did, over seven months later. I learned to be very careful what you pray for. Nick came out of coma—blind, 80 lbs. thinner, with no finger use, unable to walk or talk and with short-term memory loss.

I spent the next twenty-six years praying with Nick for him to see and reminded Nick many times that God answered that prayer by granting him the gift of seeing a piece of Heaven. I know the truth of this because I was privileged with the opportunity to see Nick overwhelmed with joy at the rapture of what he saw. I spent years trying to get my camera out in time to capture the look on his face before it faded back to normal.

One day, at age 29, Nick asked me how old he was and I told him. His response was to spell the word "old" out in the air. Yet, later, he was so glad to turn 40 because he was sure that he had the wisdom to accompany the age—and he did—and so do you Gail.

I watched my son discover a miracle—Nick walking. Pete, at age five, was in the convalescent home watching as Nick stood in a walker with four people surrounding him and took a few steps. Pete stated, "Look Mom, it's a miracle!" I realized at that moment it was, but not the miracle I thought I had prayed for.

I look back on how we walked with Nick holding on to our shoulders and limping along till he finally got his brace and could walk as I prayed for. I thank God everyday that he gave Nick what he wanted most. Mom asked Nick if he could see, walk or talk, what would he want most. Nick said "walk" and he got it— thank you Lord.

Nick had a walking bar in his living room that he could walk around while I read to him. I would read, and he would listen to, a book a week and the Bible in between.

He had another walking bar on his back porch, which he and I used to enjoy the weather and listen to music and talk: family, politics, religion and everything in between. His yard had chipmunks and they would walk past him knowing they were safe if he was walking. Any other activity on the porch and the chipmunks would scurry by. His yard is filled with birds. We tried to identify the birds by sound with him but never succeeded.

Because of Nick, Peter will not fight. Peter grew up knowing what could happen in a fight. But Nick's greatest influence on Peter is his relationship with Jesus. Peter witnessed miracles at a young age and learned how to pray and how to forgive. You can't spend time with Nick and not pray. You can't spend time with Nick and not think about your relationship with God.

God is Nick's first thought. The phrase "what would Jesus do" was his way of living. You can't be around Nick and not admire his faith and strength of character. He makes you realize how much you take for granted. Nick takes nothing for granted.

My children, Peter and Amy, grew up watching Nick's rehabilitation: the struggle it took, the hours a day spent at it, the progress he made, how slow it all was, the courage their uncle had and the spirit that would not quit.

Pete struggled to help Nick play catch with him. He finally got a *nerf* ball that Nick could squeeze and try to throw. Nick could finally hold a ball, reach his arm back to throw it but it just fell to the ground. By the time our nephew Kyle was old enough to play catch, Nick could hold a regular baseball, without it popping out of his hand and throw it to Kyle.

My daughter Amy spent her preschool years in a convalescent home with elderly people as her playmates. She learned a sense of compassion there that has been with her ever since. I admire how she has defended and fought for people who aren't what the world considers "beautiful" and now she is signing at her church for the deaf. I believe Nick had something to do with this. Amy decorated Nick's long-leg brace with stickers, which inspired my mother to make his final brace very colorful.

Nicole is Nick's namesake and has shared a life and love with him that very few know. Nick just puts out his arm and Nicole comes for her hug. She made a point of sharing everything in her life with him and he loved every moment of it. She was the child he did not get to have but he got to help raise her in a very special way. Any conversation about Nicole made Nick smile. Gail St. Mary, Nick's aide, is the best friend anyone can have and we are so blessed that she was Nick's. She patiently worked for years with Nick to walk and talk. She too shared her adult life with Nick and shared all that was going on in their lives. Her kids never spoke baby talk because she taught them how to speak correctly as soon as they could make sounds. Her children have been devoted to Nick and loved like his own.

As anyone who has had their lives dramatically changed knows, the anniversary of the date of their injury and their birthdays always bring out so many feelings—and anger is a big one. Yet, I have been amazed at how many other things will bring back the pain over what happened.

A man tried to kill my brother with a baseball bat in a YMCA. God did not do it, a man did it. This man needs to be acknowledged for what he did. He was trying to kill Nick and 26 years and 327 days later he did. He is about to go on trial for assaulting another man in front of his 6 year old son. Nick wanted to be in court when he is sentenced. My family and I will be there for him.

Nick's death certificate could have said homicide and we could have pressed new charges. It was very tempting.

Nick lived blind for 26 years and 327 days with a severe TBI. He was the most amazing person I have ever known. Nick forgave this man and it took me years after Nick to be able to do that. But that does not mean I am not angry over all of it. I forgave him for me, not for him; he doesn't know it and never will.

"A Man" To Remember

I had to move past the hatred and bitterness in order to live my life and be the person I want to be. But that takes time and as anyone who has been through the process knows, you need to work through it all to get there.

There comes a time when you feel the anger but it doesn't affect you anymore, if that makes sense. The anger is about what has happened to my brother's life and my family's life. It is all about what could have and should have been. When you can begin to count the blessings TBI brings into your life, it gets better. I can tell you that the blessings are more than the hurts and time really does heal a lot of wounds, but not all.

Nick helped me raise my children and knew what was going on in their lives, every day of their lives. He would have been a stricter parent than I was but his advice along the way gave me the help I needed to give them what they needed.

God knew Nick was going to be blind and gave him the time and opportunity to see the Grand Canyon, fly over the ocean, motorcycle through the desert and scuba dive in the ocean. He saw the four seasons of New England and the faces of my children.

Nick has taught me how to listen and hear, even though my husband Tom may not always think so.

Nick taught his nieces and nephews how to spell, do math, play kick ball at his walking bar, the joy and value of a hug—and always corrected any child who did not mind his mother.

Nick was with me picking up Amy from high school. She

had reserved a video of a movie she wanted to see. Nick was in the front passenger seat and Amy was in the back seat while I went into the store to pick up the movie. As I came out of the store, Nick had his mouth open and his eyes were as big as saucers. This was not a look I was familiar with. I asked Amy what they were talking about. She said he wanted to know about the movie she was getting. It was about a crazy uncle who gets out of a mental hospital and comes back and tries to kill his niece—*Nightmare on Elm Street*. His reaction to this and his expression said it all.

Nick, after assault, and with a TBI, was not an easy man to know because he spoke so slowly and it required time to get to know him in his new body. Few people would take the time. Through this, Nick taught me patience and appreciation for what is really important. The best thing I learned from Nick's example is how to accept people for who they are and not who you want them to be. He was great at it and I know I will never be as good.

Most of all, Nick taught me what real faith, real trust and real love are all about. Not the kind that is preached about, but the kind you live. He never doubted God, he just trusted Him completely and loved like a child. "Unless you have faith like this, you cannot enter the kingdom of heaven." Nick had the courage and strength to live with many handicaps  and never complain. We did share many tears about being blind, holding hands, head to head, and talking about it. He gave 100% in all he did. He put what God would want him to do first in every thought and action.

Nick and I enjoyed many concerts, mostly the *Moody Blues*. An "Oldies" concert was at a casino with slot machines, great food and a wonderful show. He was a different person at these shows and loved them. He always shocked people when he could not sit any longer and had to get out of the wheel chair and get up and dance.

Nick spent the last birthday of his life in a hospital. It was the only birthday he ever spent in a hospital. His birthday is December 20th. December was always a hard month for Nick after injury; all of the decorations he could not see, the excitement, the joy and the happiness. Too much was going on at once. Now he was very sick and was in the hospital for two weeks. He made it home for Christmas and made it through the day with us and had a wonderful time.

But, it was the first time he did not get better. He bounced back from everything before. Maybe not 100%, but he rebounded. By February, he was back in the hospital. We knew he was not getting better but Mom, Gail and I decided to wait for spring. Nick always gets better in the spring we said. The good weather and new life all around always helped him. Spring came and he was not getting better. He was weaker, losing weight, and breathing was so much harder. He could barely talk at a whisper. It was taking two people to transfer Nick and his physical care was taking a toll on everyone. Mom and Dad put in *barrier free lifts* so one person could take care of him and it gave Nick the opportunity to get back in his Jacuzzi.

After two trips to the emergency room to help

Nick breathe, we had to face reality. Mom and I went to see Nick's doctor and talk about what is reality. Nick was dying. Dad, Mom and I discussed the options available and decided to talk to Nick and let him make his own decision.

If there is another lesson to be learned by Nick's life, it is how to handle dying. I ran a conference at my church with a panel discussion about people dying and how to help people talk about it and make their wishes known to those they love and who will be stuck making the decisions.

Nick, thank you for wanting me to be a part in making your decisions. Thank you for helping Gail to accept them. I think Nick was glad to hear in words what he already knew—his imminent death. Now all of us would be able to deal with it. He comforted me when we discussed it. There is such peace knowing the person you love has lived a life that will give him so much reward in the next. But the letting go is so very difficult.

I could not say goodbye. I could only tell Nick that I love him and it is ok to go. Mom, Dad, Gail, Debbie V., Theresa, Nicole and I were with Nick for his last hours. We prayed, we talked, we sang and we held hands. His last word was "Alleluia".

Although he suffered for months before his death, he did die in peace and was surrounded by the people who loved him so very much. May I know that much love at my time of death.

Nick lived as his therapist once put it—with one foot in heaven and one foot on earth and never quite knowing where he wanted to be.

Nick's life was truly blessed by our good Lord

and I was given the privilege of witnessing so many miracles. Nick's life also helps you appreciate the miracles we tend to take for granted. We were blessed with having no regrets and nothing left unsaid. I do trust God and know it was Nick's time to go. He also has shown me great comfort in my grief. I often told Nick he has more friends in heaven than he does on earth and that there was going to be quite a party to celebrate his arrival.

Nick, your death has had a powerful effect on my life. At times I am doing fine. I am trying to find out what normal is and I have no idea. People tell me I can fulfill my dreams now. My kids are raised, I have grandkids I love and have the chance to really enjoy. I have a job I like most of the time and I have a husband who loves me and has stood by me through all that has happened for 33 years.

But you, my dear brother, taught me everyday what is important and I am in many ways lost without you. I am angry at people who complain. I want to shout to the world that I lost the best part of my life, a huge part of me, and no one knows what that means or what it is like. We have buried so many people; most of our aunts and uncles, a nephew, and my mother-in-law. No one's passing has affected me like this. I went to your grave last night and told you I didn't mean it when I said it was okay to go. I do need you. I can't talk to anyone the way I talked to you. You know me—and my whole life—and never judged anything but always gave me blunt, straight answers and advice.

I can't stop thinking about the day you died. I didn't want you to suffer anymore but I don't want life without you. The physical burden of caring for you is easy to let go of, but the rest of you, the spirit that is you, is missed so much. The house is so quiet. It has been weeks now and I am expected to be back to normal but every time I have a minute to myself, I am on the verge of tears. The ache of pain is so real. You are my morning prayers, my breakfast chitchat, and the beginning of everyday. You are the one I stop to see when things are tough for either one of us. You are the only person in my life who could get me to talk about what was bothering me when I normally keep it in. You knew before anyone else when something was off, all the time. I cherish how you would not do what I wanted until I did what you wanted.

Nick, thanks for the good feelings about cleaning out your stuff and the flowers you sent our way. They helped. We certainly don't need things to keep you in our thoughts and hearts. I do enjoy all the plants and you are making it a challenge to keep them all alive. You'd better help me there. I like the idea of the "life after life" that they represent. Your life will live on in your book. As you know, many more people are reading it and being affected by it.

I attended one of the Masses offered for you today at St. John's Church. I passed the handicapped parking where we always parked and remembered the rainy day we almost didn't get to go to church. You prayed and the rain stopped. We counted on your prayers for the good weather after that and you are still answering them. I remembered the teacher who came up to us after she saw you walk into the church after years of the wheel chair. She had been praying for you and was so happy to see you walking and her prayers being answered.

You were always so surprised on learning that people were praying for you. I do hope Joseph Tramontano goes back to jail and the other victim of his madness doesn't give up. I will be there every day of the trial, for you, and also for me. I do wish you could have made it to his sentencing. You deserved that. I will try to remember that God will be his judge and it is not so important in the scheme of things.

You were very blessed in not having to deal with the earthly burdens of everyday life. The handicaps were not worth it but it did give you the time and opportunity to grow into the magnificent human being you were and the great saint you are now. I don't have that luxury but will try to accomplish a degree of it.

You had choices and sure gave us a great example of how to choose right. I feel like I have choices now but I am not sure what they are. I still ache for you. I miss your advice, your courage and your sparkling eyes.

4

Mary D'Agata, Friend and Nurse

Mary D'Agata was the nurse on duty at Kimberly Hall in 1977 when Nick first arrived there after leaving the intensive care at the hospital. It was Mary, and a few others like her, that made it possible for us to leave our son in their care and not go completely out of our minds with worry.

Mary turned out to be more than a nurse—she became our very dear friend. She loved Nick and took more than a special interest in him. He loved her and would wind his way out of his room in a wheel chair and listen for her voice. Then, blind, and not knowing how to get to her, he would listen again for her voice and somehow wheel his chair around the nurse's station and come to sit beside her.

On June 3, 1979, Mary sent us a thank you card. She finally left Kimberly Hall to further her education and spend more time with her family.

Dear Barbara & John,

How can I express my feelings for Nick and all of you? Getting to know such remarkable people and nursing "back to life" such a <u>beautiful</u> person has been <u>the</u> most outstanding experience in my years of nursing.

Leaving Kimberly Hall after over 4 years was difficult but leaving Nick to someone else's care bothered me much more. I'm sure, in the long run, it is a good thing—he must learn to deal with new people & not rely on old ties too much.

Ann Smith is one of the best nurses I know—caring and very knowing. She'll do a fine job.

Thanks for your gifts—they are very special to me. Please keep in touch. I hope our friendship is on more than a professional level!

Fondly,
Mary D'Agata

Mary sent a short note on September 12, 1979:

Dear Barbara,

Ronnie told me you called about 1 week later. I've been so busy with school. Please call again. I'm home most of the weekend & suppertime during the week.

Nick was so good today. Good memory & responses. Knew what Anthropology (one of my courses) was about! Hope we can visit soon.
Mary

Through incidents like this we were learning that Nick's mind and memory were far better than any doctor ever gave us hope it would be. She sent me another letter dated October 2, 1979.

Dear Barbara,

Today it occurred to me that it's been just about 2 years since we met—quite an unusual friendship. A strange coincidence—as you know I've been at school taking the old basic English Comp.101. The professor's theory—take pen in hand and begin writing words. I have writer's cramp, believe me!

"A Man" To Remember

Last week I was thinking of Nick and you, as I so often do. My pen was ready so I began writing. Believe me—I've never written poetry—essays are my line—I'm enclosing what came of my effort—not too much effort. I hope you'll like it and understand. Share it if you like.

To Nick—Two Years Later

Brain jellied by a baseball bat
There he sits,
Eyes vibrantly alive
But unseeing
He tramps thru my heart
Quiet, but demanding
Love; his unspoken but freely given.

Changes wrought by circumstance,
A young man's life
Full, now empty
But for the love, the caring
His very presence demands.

The cacophony unbearable,
Insane confusion enveloping:
Could one choose—deaf or blind.
Death or life
Unfulfilled?

Cruel God, where is the purpose?
Will he live to understand?
The fulfillment lies in others'
Spirits growing day by day;
Enriched by his example
Of fortitude, love, forgiveness.

"A Man" To Remember

Mary captured Nick's life and purpose so beautifully in her little English composition poem. It has always meant a great deal to me.

Nick received a letter from Mary dated February 13, 1981.

Dear Nick,

Just thought I'd write to let you know I still think of you, and your great family. They are very special people, as you well know, and, of course, you're one of the specialest!

Nick, your Mom called to wish me a Merry Christmas and let me know how you're doing. I wasn't very happy to hear that one of the greatest eaters of all time is now on a liquid tube feeding—not much fun! My son, Tom, is the only one I know that appreciates a fine meal as much as you do.

Do you remember how you and I used to talk about food?—different kinds of cookies was always a good topic of conversation. Lobster, another! If I could never have another lobster I'd always remember how it feels to sit on a rocky beach in Maine, with the sky bluer than anywhere in the world—with the cold waves crashing the rocks and a million lobster-pot markers bobbing on the water only a few feet from shore. That's where I've eaten the best lobster, cooked right in sea-water, and I'll never forget how it tastes— we didn't even need the butter. I guess you have a lot of food memories too.

Hope you like the new place you live at. It's nice that your family can get in more often to visit. I'm sure both they, and you, like that! You were ready for a change—we all need to move once in a while, and it's good fun meeting new people—most of them are great, aren't they?

Hope your mom keeps in touch with me; a postcard would do. Keep smiling, Nick! I think of you often.

Love, as always

Mary D'Agata

This was the last correspondence we had with Mary. How ironic it is that she should have died before Nick! But can you imagine the reunion these two shared when he arrived in Heaven!

5

Kevin Trembley, Friend and Sailor

In 1980 a young sailor visiting a seminary near Kimberly Hall, (where Nick was taken after leaving ICU and the hospital setting), befriended Nick. His name is Kevin Trembley. I have kept his letters all these years because he was such a rare human being who met another rare human being. They formed a bond that comes through in these letters even though Nick could not speak.

These letters are a treasure and will show how early on after his injury Nick was able to have a dramatic influence on the lives of people who came in contact with him. Kevin voluntarily took Nick for walks at Kimberly Hall and talked with him endlessly. He surely has to be one of those angels Nick thought was coming to take him out of hell—into Heaven! Perhaps God did send him.

We lost contact with Kevin and efforts to locate him failed. What a loss! Kevin, you, too, are a man to remember for your wonderful caring, thoughtfulness, inspiration and devotion to Nick. Thank you.

I have taken excerpts from some of his letters:

Saturday, November 29, 1980

Dear Nick,

The holiday season has arrived and I've finally gotten around to dropping you a letter. First, let me say I hope I find you in the very best of spirits!

I last saw you in October—I don't know if you remember but, I told you then that I had come up from Virginia to visit a seminary that was only a few miles away from you & I figured since I was so close I would drop in & say hello to you first & ask for a couple of prayers too. So that's about where we left off.

Let me brief you on what I'm up to, ok? Last summer I used to visit you as often as I could & take you for a walk around Kimberly Hall. We'd pick blackberries & blueberries & stuff & have an all around nice afternoon together. By the way, did anyone tell you lately that you're great company? Well, you are. Anyway, being as I'm in the navy—it's their option to give me a transfer—as you know from the Air Force. They did that. Right to Norfolk, Virginia.

I can remember I was very down about that—I had friends like you & your family in Connecticut. I was able to live at home. And, to top it all off, I had to cancel a retreat I had scheduled with the Trappists!!! When I left the area for Virginia, you were the last person I visited. I took the highway going by Kimberly to go to Virginia just for that purpose. It was early when I stopped in—you were still in bed! I asked for your prayers again. Boy I'm always asking you for prayers!

Well! They were answered, (as always when God feels the time is right.) I was no sooner down here for a week or two until I was referred by a chaplain to Holy Family Retreat House. He said I could make a good retreat there. Was he right? I've been living here ever since!

For a couple of weeks I visited here every day—helped paint & all—they were painting the whole place by way of volunteers. I'd eat supper with them & pray after. Then, at about 10 or so I'd go to the base & sleep there. After a while I just ended up with a room at the House & there I sleep now!

To make a long & beautiful story short, we are now working on getting me out of the contract which binds me until May of 1984 to the Navy. The seminary has declared me acceptable & they are behind me. So Nick, you can perceive I'm going to ask you for more prayers, huh? We have a long way to go yet. But, as you know, 'If God is for us, who can stand against us?'

I have many friends who encourage me—like yourself & your family. I even have a man I know in the hospital—his name is Bobby.

I guess it was in his senior year of high school (prom night I think but I'm not sure) that he was in a terrible accident. The nuns have been taking care of him ever since. His problem is similar to yours for his body, but he can see and speak. He's been in the hospital longer than I have been alive & he never seems to complain. He loves God very much too & that has helped him greatly. There are so many wonderful people aren't there Nick? Each with their own gifts.

Take the Greatest of Care & I hope this letter brightens your days a little bit!

May God Bless You!

Kevin

By the time Kevin's next letter arrived Nick had left Kimberly Hall and was in a nursing home in Watertown.

Sunday, March 29, 1981

Dear Mary,

Thank you for telling me of Nick's move and present condition. I'm glad he's so much closer to his family members now—it's so important to have support. I'm sure it means almost everything to him.

Over the last couple of months my ship (and I) have been down in the Caribbean Sea. We had ships exercises in & around Guantanamo Bay, Cuba, Roosevelt Road, Puerto Rico. We visited the Bahamas (Nassau). A place called Fredrickstead on the island of St. Croix in the Virgin Islands and a French colony called Martinique, which is getting closer to Venezuela. It's one of those little Islands north of South America. Visiting all of these places I realized how lucky I have it in the U.S. Sure there were nice tourist attractions but once you walk past you see how poor the natives of the island live. It then becomes easy to understand why they try & capitalize on the tourist trade so much.

The faith of these islanders is Catholic and strong. I was very glad to perceive that. Also, even though their children are so poor they go to fairly nice Catholic schools & they're well educated & all. The boys & girls each have their little uniforms. I think now if I won a trip to an island from some game show I'd look at it in a different light altogether.

You can read this letter to Nick of course & tell

him he is constantly in my special intentions when the priests offer the prayers of the faithful during the mass & I keep a little notebook calendar that I write my rosary intentions in & I often put Nick's name & then say the rosary for him asking Our dearest & most loving Mother for her special help, prayers, intercession & especially the comfort only she can bring. The greatest gift she has to give us is her divine love for her son. If only we could love with the love that she does. And yes, she too had to (& indeed still does) suffer.

Remember too Nick, that St. Paul (who was knocked off his horse by Jesus on the road to Damascus) had an affliction in his body, often suffered at the hands of others too. He rejoiced in his suffering because he knew he was joining his own with that of Jesus for the good of mankind & the salvation of his soul & the souls of others. He wanted to die at times but he wanted to show love for Jesus even more & did!

Your love for Our Jesus is an inspiration to me Nick, and to many others. The men of the world would say you have no reason to love God. But, you are not of this world Nick & because of that the world doesn't really know you any more than they knew Jesus. Jesus says that & loves you because of that. All the more does He love you for the souls you are saving by your own pains. Be confident & know you are doing good just by being Nick Del Buono.
God love you.

God Bless you, your husband, loved ones & the rest of the Del Buono family.

Love, Kevin

"A Man" To Remember

This is one of Kevin's last notes to Nick in the form of a Christmas card.

Dear Nick,

It has been an awful long time since last I saw you in person but as I look back upon this year past & recall the things I have to be thankful for I know that the beauty of the present depends upon the impressions from the past. Nick, your life is a gift. I try & try and pierce the depths of the mystery of suffering & difficulty. Too deep is it for me to understand but to the spirit it's a healing balm. Your trials have been my lesson—a teacher who could not speak to me in words. A gift far greater than any gold, frankincense and myrrh, you have shared yourself. May God be continually pleased to bless you always.

Praying for a happy, holy & blessed Christmas for you & your family.

Love,
Kevin
(a sailor for a few months more!)

6

Gail St. Mary, Friend and Aide

Over the twenty-one years that Nick lived at home it was necessary to hire many aides to help with his care. I also hired a speech pathologist, a physical therapist, an occupational therapist and a massage therapist to work with Nick and instruct all of us in the proper care and rehabilitation of Nick.

But it was the aides who were most important in Nick's life and ours. A few became so close and stayed so long with Nick that they became like daughters to us. Gail St. Mary was a young eighteen-year-old teenager when she started working with Nick in 1982, when he was still in a nursing home.

When he came home to live, she came with him. She was his coach and he was her champ. They spent almost twenty-two years together. Nick attended and danced at her wedding, held her hand and her stomach as her first child was born, cried, and was the impetus for saving her life when that child died after only a few months of life, was there for her as she had three more children and became their Uncle Nick. He  counseled her through a very difficult divorce and loved her dearly to the day he died.

The friendship that developed between them would be hard to describe, but maybe Gail can do that much better than I ever could. Gail will always be like one of our daughters and her children our adopted grandchildren for the rest of our lives.

Gail is one of the reasons why we are so glad that Nick lived. If he had not, we would never have met this wonderful person and her children. Oh! What we would have missed! It is another way in which Nick's life has been so meaningful and has blessed so many other people.

This is Gail's story about Nick

On July 5, 1982 I met an incredible man who changed my life forever. At eighteen years old what did I know? Not much, compared to now. Twenty-two years of "working" is how I met an angel here on earth.

I was working as a home health aide and was called to take a job with a patient who was lying helpless in a nursing home bed who had been traumatically brain-injured. I had no training with brain injury and only six months training with geriatric patients. Yet I spontaneously said I could do this job.

The nurse told me of his needs and his condition. But not one word was spoken about the patient himself, his personality, his likes or dislikes or his abilities or lack of them. Looking back, if any person or caretaker "working" with Nick took the time to really "know" him and look inside at his soul, they would have found a man with the patience of a saint, a never-ending love of God, and a love of life with the greatest will to live that I have ever seen before.

"A Man" To Remember

What a shame that the people working with Nick at the nursing home didn't take the time to get to know Nick. Oh! What they missed!

Over the years with helpful stories from family and ideas and suggestions to help me know Nick better and be more personal I got to know the man inside the body that was so crippled. I wanted to know him and not just his medical and personal hygiene needs.

All my life I thought I was not judgmental on appearances as a sighted person until I met Nick. Witnessing him meeting people, he met a person soul to soul and not body to body. His way of meeting a person was different and the real way we should all meet new people. This way he got to know the "real" person. He didn't care if you were tall or short, skinny or fat (unless you were going to cut your hair—he always wanted women to have long hair). It was always amazing to me how when his mother came into a room he would tell her she looked pretty. His compliments were just awesome.

I think the most phenomenal and most impressive thing that I found about him—not just the spirituality—not that he existed, but that he truly "lived" here on earth. We talked about this often. How people go about their day-to-day activities and don't notice all the things going on about them.

"A Man" To Remember

But Nick truly wanted to know everything he could about life. When it came time to eat—he wanted to know about food and cooking. When he went outside he wanted to know everything he could about plants and trees. Nick truly knew how to stop and smell the roses—all of them.

The gazebo in the back yard was our heaven on earth. It had a swing in it and we made it to that place no matter what it took to get there. Mom had a latch put on the foot of the swing so that we could have it hold still until he mounted the floor of the swing. Most of the time we got there by angels' wings. Nick wanted to swing as high as it would go and I think I was the only one who would go that high with him because everyone else  would get sick. It was the most peaceful place on earth. We read books and talked about the seasons and sometimes spent two hours just swinging back and forth.

When Mom and Dad would take a vacation we decided we would take a vacation too. We would put up posters from wherever we wanted to go. We cooked food from that place and even put wrappers around the soap that would indicate where we were. We went to Mexico, Ireland, Italy and England—all the while staying at home and enjoying every moment.

Nick and I went to movies together and I always

"A Man" To Remember

wondered how he could handle this. It was difficult because he had to wear a leg bag to collect his urine, get in a wheel chair, and then "see" a movie he couldn't see. We did the same with concerts. Nick's attitude was that he was going to enjoy being at these events no matter what it took to get there. He just seemed to find ways to make a bad situation the best it could be. He very rarely would be at a party and say he was upset and wanted to leave, despite not being able to see the people there, and often, the gifts they were opening.

I just wish I could put into words how I feel about Nick but I can't. There are no words to describe how I felt around him. His example here on earth cannot be touched. I have never felt the likes of it before. His way of dealing with things and trusting were examples of how to live that I do not believe I will ever encounter again.

Nick taught me how to live—and how to die. I am the person who got to my brother's funeral and couldn't go in the church when I was twelve years old. My brother would have been thirteen in two more weeks. When my first-born child died I was asked if I wanted to go in the room to see him. I couldn't go in the room. Death was associated with tragedy all of my life. It was only  when Nick died that I learned that death was a part of life and that it could be beautiful. I never imagined that I could be holding hands with someone who was dying but Nick guided me through this difficult time with his trust and love for God.

"Trust in God" is what he always said when dealing with troubles here on Earth. I would often push this "trust in God" statement to the back of my mind and think of a "real" solution to my problem.

In my younger days, I found myself doing this often when Nick and I would discuss things. I was never ignoring his advice, I just didn't have a lot of faith.

As years went by I seemed to have a different "feeling" around Nick. It was like a spiritual "aura" was around us. I found myself turning to Nick to pray with because he seemed extremely close to God. I have never felt that way being around anyone else. It always felt as if Nick had "connections" with God, that I didn't.

Nick unconditionally loved everyone that I witnessed him meet. His first introduction to a new friend was, "I love you," or a kiss on their hand. How many people DARE do that. But that's Nick's style—to love and do God's will. I think if he could he would wash your feet. His example on how to live makes me believe without a doubt that he was a unique saint here on Earth. He proved to the world that NO MATTER WHAT God is behind all that we do, ONLY if we TRUST and let Him in our lives, asking God to bless us with grace everyday and being humble.

When Nick did not feel well, he prayed. When being told of a person's illness or death, Nick immediately made the Sign of the Cross and started praying to God (and his lips were moving). He shone in church—like being home with God. Babies were always called miracles. He was always asking me if he could help me do anything. He constantly forgot he was injured. He always said, "God will help me". He never worried about anything—except making it to Heaven.

And Nick, I have no doubt whatsoever that you are there and enjoying every minute of it.

Goodbye to earth, my champ.

Gail St. Mary

7

Gail's Sons

Brandon Duffany is Gail's youngest son. He is a nine-year-old, extremely handsome young man and more than an "honor" student. He has already skipped one grade and may have to skip another because of his inclination to the genius class.

Spencer Duffany is Gail's middle son. He is eleven years old, charming, loving, and a very good student too. Spencer is that child that snuggles his way into your heart and you cannot help but love him. Nick had a special affection for Spencer.

Zachary Duffany is thirteen years old now and the child who saved Gail's life after her first-born child Marty died when he was only a few months old. Zachary is a very sensitive young man who is much bigger than his years would lead you to believe. But he is a real teddy bear of a person and one of the best cooks in the world. He is the one who gave "Grandpa Dude" his name when he saw John dressed up in a cowboy outfit when he was just a small boy. Grandpa Dude loves Zachary's sausage and peppers and Zachary too.

All three of these boys were and are frequent visitors in our home. Each one learned to love their "Uncle Nick" and he loved them back. As soon as he would hear their voices, his left arm would extend and they would be enveloped in a big hug.

Nick was a disciplinarian. Any exhibit of bad behavior from any child would bring his swift

"A Man" To Remember

admonitions. He absolutely insisted that each child respect his or her mother. No word of sass could be said in front of him that was not reprimanded.

Gail taught her children to understand the word "handicapped" in a way that most children never get to know. They never treated Nick as though he were "different" from any other person. This was a great gift to these children and one that will follow them all the days of their lives.

Nick's death affected all three of her son's deeply. Caught up in our own grief, we sometimes did not think about what the children were going through. Many weeks after Nick's death, Gail found a note and diagram under Brandon's pillow. I think it explains the depth of his feelings:

My uncle could not use the muscle to stop his food from going into his lungs. He had brain damage. And on May, 18, 2004 he perished because of this activity.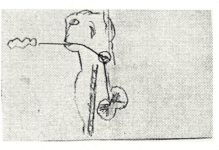

I am in a very, very, bad mood and I am really sad.

Later, Brandon was able to write about his feelings for Nick:

When I first met my Uncle Nick I saw that he was brain-damaged but after I knew him it felt like he was a very special, extraordinary man. I didn't notice he was handicapped.

But one thing I will remember about him is that he is the best player when we played *Yahtzee*. He was also good at trivia questions, or pretty much any board games.

One thing I really enjoyed is when my Mom read to him on the gazebo. We used to go outside all of the time.

I feel so bad for him now. Every day he would say his prayers to God to give him a better life. That life is in Heaven and I pray for him now. I pray that God gives him the life he had before the incident.

When I go to Heaven I will get to see my Uncle Nick. I, too, will live a better life in Heaven with Saint Nick.

Spencer wrote the following note about Nick:

My Uncle Nick was like a dove to me. He flew higher than anything. He loved and cared for anyone with all his heart. He and I were very close. He would hold my hand if I were hurt. He would take me into his arms and hug me tight.

In Heaven I will play with him, talk to him and walk with him and even go on a cloud gazebo like we did on earth.

I miss him very much.
Spencer

"A Man" To Remember

Zachary's sensitivity comes through loud and clear in his statement about Nick:

What I am about to write about my uncle cannot be expressed without crying. My Uncle Nick was my inspiration and is someone who I will always remember. He was the hero of a lifetime and is a hero of my dreams.

He backed me up even when I was wrong and then he would tell me in the most soothing words where I went wrong. He might have been blind and not able to remember things but he was considered a saint in my eyes.

At night I think about him and cry for hours. When he died I couldn't bear the news of what had happened. When I think about him it is hard to breathe. He will remain in our hearts forever while he enjoys Heaven.

He made this family very proud to see him rise to Heaven and take the pain away—not only from him but from a family that cares the most.

Zachary

8

Carly Fenn, Friend and Aide

A woman answered an ad that I had placed in the newspaper for an aide to help Nick. She couldn't take the job but told me about a friend of hers who would like to have an interview. I quickly agreed to meet with her friend as I needed help with Nick's care. Carly Fenn was the young lady who came into our home and joined the select group who Nick considered his angels on earth.

She was just the person I was looking for to help him. She was young and strong and very personable. She was not the least bit shy about taking care of him and she was a pleasant conversationalist. He needed that. It was dreadful for him to sit in a room, blind, with a person who did not communicate well and often.

Over the years Carly became a friend to all of the family, especially our granddaughter Nicole. She teased "Mr. D" unmercifully and he loved it. She was kind and considerate of me in every situation and that, too, is an admirable quality. To have strangers in your home from early morning to late at night seven days a week can be very intrusive if they are not the kind of people who fit in well with the atmosphere in the home.

Carly was and is a gem and we not only didn't mind having her in our home—we looked forward to her coming each day. We hated the time when vacation rolled around because we would be without her charm and personality for longer than we wanted to be.

Nick loved Carly deeply and she returned his affection. She knew his likes and dislikes and catered to him always. They played music, sang songs, listened to TV programs and danced together as friends. She stayed with Nick for ten years. But I should let Carly tell you of her own experience with Nick.

A Tribute To My Lifetime Angel

Let me begin by letting every person who reads this know that John Nicholas Del Buono is, was and always will be the most remarkable human being I have ever met. Do you know anybody who wakes up daily and proclaims his love to God and Life? Nick would open his beautiful eyes (that were able to see only heavenly beauty, not earthly beauty) and say, "I see God, I see Heaven?", "I Love life!" and/or "God and Heaven are working on me!"

Nick, you are so right buddy—life is now lived with God and Heaven at your side blessing your eyes, mind, body and soul for all eternity. All the years robbed of your earthly vision(s) you now have all the glorious angels with their long hair and golden wings fluttering around you at all times.

I loved when you would tell me about the angels you were seeing, about their beautiful flowing locks of hair and their golden wings. I can only imagine what they looked like.

Nick, I miss you more than you can imagine. You are in my thoughts and prayers daily. I miss your big bear hugs everyday and the way you would kiss my hand like only a gentleman would. I miss your big beautiful smile and your wisdom and wit. I learned a lot about life and God from you. Thank you for being my friend, my teacher and my lifetime angel.

I listen to the *Moody Blues* from time to time and I wish we could have gone to one more concert with Mary. I reminisce of the hours you and I spent walking around your bar with the music blasting, or the times we would just sit and listen.

Nick, I thank you from the bottom of my heart for all the years of loyal friendship, your caring ways and for being the man you are.

To all who read this and were able to know Nick, you are a very lucky person. For those who never had the opportunity to meet Nick, I wish you had because your life would have been touched by a very remarkable man and a real life angel!

Nick, I know you are up in Heaven smiling down on us. I want you to know that I hope to one day meet up with you again. Until then, you will remain by my side and in my heart, my friend.

Thank you for being my friend and touching my soul as you have.

With much love
Carly

"A Man" To Remember

Wings of an Angel

A gentle wind blew cross the land,
Reaching out to take a hand

For on the winds the angel came,
Calling out my friend Nick's name.

Left behind, with our tears,
Loving memories of the years.

Of joy and love, a life well spent,
And now to God you were sent.

On angel's wings, a heavenly flight,
The journey home, towards the light.

To those who weep, a life is gone,
But in God's love, 'tis but the dawn.

Carly Fenn

9

Debra Vienneau, Friend and Aide

Another young woman came into our lives in 1986 and she brought us great joy as she lovingly took care of our son. Her name is Debra Vienneau and it is a name that Nick learned quickly and never forgot. As soon as Debbie would walk in a room and ask him who she was, he would reply, "Debbie Vienneau." Maybe this doesn't sound like much of an accomplishment, but you must remember that Nick was blind and had to learn the name of each new person who worked with him by voice inflection alone. He couldn't do this with everyone, but he did with Debbie.

She brought her charm, her out-going personality and intense devotion to Nick and filled his life with a very special kind of enjoyment and pleasure. She studied to become a medical technician while working with Nick and he often helped her with her homework. Sometimes he knew the answer to a question when she didn't.

After graduating and finding a job in the field she had chosen, she returned on her one day off each week to work with Nick because she didn't want to lose touch with him and he enjoyed these days very much. She became his "omelet queen" as she put everything she could find in the cabinets and refrigerator to make these dishes special for him to eat and enjoy.

Debbie's story with Nick is another very special one and only she can tell it properly. She loves to write poetry and following is one I found that she wrote just after she started working with Nick in 1986. He did have a way of making a quick and lasting impression.

"NICK"

I started helping a man I knew nothing about.
But 5 minutes with Nick — my heart went out.

I talk with him and walk with him
and read him stories.
You can see in his face all his expressions
and his glories.

Sometimes we just sit and relax for a while
But we all know Nick is thinking
"This is not my style."

He loves walking on his bars
and doing speech therapy.
When I'm with Nick,
there is no place I'd rather be.

Just getting to know Nick,
you are well on your way
Of knowing he is so special
and will sure make your Day!

"A Man" To Remember

After Nick died Debbie wrote another poem and a letter for Nick.

A Poem from the Heart — In Loving Memory

Nick
Son — Brother — Best Friend

How do I handle the loss of you, the pain that plagues me daily —

How do I cope with tears that fall, wishing I could run to you for a hug —

How does my heart stop hurting when I hear our favorite songs —

Who do I share my inner-most thoughts with and not be judged —

Who do I go and talk to for advice and get the most loving answers —

Because of You

I handle the loss of you with all of the strength you have given me —

I cope with the tears because of all the hugs and smiles I was so blessed to get —

I listen to our favorite songs with a heart that is so full of love for you —

I still share my thoughts with you because I know you are listening —

And I smile to myself because I heard everything you have ever said to me —

I handle my pain over losing you by the blessing of having you in my life—

You are gone from earth but never forgotten because of who you are—

All I will ever have to do is look up to the brightest star!

>Your Best Friend—Deb

>A letter to Nick
>My beloved Nick—
>My best friend

When I first answered the ad in the newspaper to care for a handicapped man, little did I know he would also be caring for me! Who would have thought that very first day of meeting each other would change my life forever.

I was young when I met Nick. I didn't know what to expect in caring for a blind, brain-injured man. I can honestly say this; he was the one who made it easy for me. Spending time with Nick just made me realize and see what an extraordinary human being he truly was.

He was never bitter with what he had to endure, the worst being his eyes. He asked God daily to have his eyesight back, but never became bitter.

Nick taught me daily how to be a better person and not take things for granted. He taught me that you do not need eyesight to see what is truly important. He had such a close and personal relationship with God and always said, "I see God working on me."

"A Man" To Remember

In the beginning I was skeptical if I may admit that. I too believe in God but that was only a fraction of how I really believe in God today, thanks to Nick. His unwavering faith got him through all of his obstacles with a positive and loving manner. Without his faith, his endeavors would have brought even the fiercest of men to their knees.

I remember all of our personal talks. Advice I would need over mistakes I have made in my life, literally crying on his shoulder and I remember each and every response—A loving hug until *he* felt it was time to let go; he always knew when I needed a hug.

Just being with him always made everything "right" again. Nick was such a strong and loving entity in my life and losing him was extremely devastating for me. I just knew I would always have Nick.

Just like the day I met Nick, came the day I had to say good-bye. He was laying on his side in his bed when I got there; Mary and Gail were also there. Mary said, "Here, Debbie, you sit with Nick." We all knew it was just a matter of time now.

So there we were, alone, just Nick and I. I am holding his hand and my nose is barely touching his. I am rubbing his head, sobbing; my heart is breaking because of the fierce love I have for this man. I begin telling him just how wonderful he is and how much we all love him. Knowing in my heart he can hear my every word.

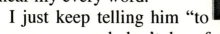

I just keep telling him "to go home now and don't be afraid because you are

"A Man" To Remember

already an angel and go toward the light!" I witnessed the most wonderful of transitions right then—Nick had passed on to Heaven as I held his hand.

So many emotions came flooding in—at first, of course, was devastation and sadness. I had just lost my best friend of eighteen years. I also felt relief for Nick because he did not have to fight anymore and now he can see!

As time passes by, I miss him in so many ways. Things we have done and our conversations together. Our favorite songs that when I hear them brings a smile to my face. One song in particular that I have always dedicated to him is *Hero* by Mariah Carey because that is Nick! A true hero in every sense of the word.

I still talk to Nick all the time and I know he is listening. I feel so truly blessed to have had Nick in my life. He truly changed me and my outlook on life.

A man that could not see and needed assistance in every aspect of daily living, taught me how to live life with love, respect and kindness. Nick has touched so many lives in such a wonderful, positive way. Losing him has been extremely difficult, but loving him has been an experience of a lifetime!

Forever—
Your loving friend
Deb—

10

Nicole Del Buono, Devoted Niece

Nicole is named for her Uncle Nick and has been his joy ever since the day she was born. Her mother was lying on the couch in the room with Nick and complaining of pains and Nick told her, "Go to the hospital, now." I accompanied my daughter and was in the delivery room when Nicole was born. What a joyous day that was!

Nicole lived the first two years of her life in our home with Nick. She was a finicky eater but when she sat in her high chair next to Nick as he was eating his meal, she would get enthusiastic about hers. She literally learned to talk listening to Nick do his  speech therapy. They formed an early bond with each other that was beautiful to watch. She remained close to him until he died.

Nicole must have inherited charm from her uncle and grandfather because she is one of the most charming persons I have ever met. She is nineteen years old now and has grown up knowing her uncle Nick like no other child. He was there for her through all of her childhood and even through her teenage years. Every prom, every dance, every special occasion was not enjoyed until she had come to get her hug from Nick.

Like all of us who were close to Nick, she has had a difficult time putting her feelings into words.

ODE 2 NICK

I'm going to make this simple
Because without him
I simply wouldn't be the person I am today.

Watching his never-ending strength
gave me the courage
to continue fighting my personal battles.

Absorbing his love taught me how to cherish one's soul and how everyone was given a spark from God.

Nick's example of a man has set a standard that others should attempt to reach.

Genuinely loving with his heart rather than his eyes was a gift that I today try to acquire.

From my first breath to his last was a fairy tale that I was fortunate enough to be a part of.

Nick's witty tongue demonstrated how a man who was labeled "incompetent" or a "vegetable" had a brain that functioned better than anyone I have ever met.

Witnessing the miracles that occurred daily at his home allowed me to trust and have faith in God.

"A Man" To Remember

God allowing Nick to be a part of my life was like winning the lotto before I was conceived.

Every loving aspect of my soul is due to him.

His one-of-a-kind character
will never, ever be replaced.

My goal in life as of May 18, 2004 is to keep his good spirit alive and teach others that God creates masterpieces—just like the work of art He created on December 20, 1951.

Love ya Nick
Nicole

11

Dr. Allen Chatt

Dr. Allen Chatt was a research associate professor of neurology at Yale University School of Medicine and a senior research psychologist at the Veterans' Administration Medical Center in West Haven, Connecticut where he was engaged in biomedical research. In 1990 he was forced into early retirement at the age of thirty-eight years due to a violent crime committed against him in 1988 which left him with multiple handicaps himself. He understood Nick's plight.

Dr. Chatt is an amazing man himself. He has worked very hard to overcome some of the most serious consequences of his injuries and still is able to help others through The Phoenix Fund for the Neurologically Challenged. He was gracious to us in that he met Nick and worked with him to try to better his life. He wrote the Foreword to my book about Nick in which he said of Nick the following words:

To know Nick Del Buono is to know "Phoenix Rising." Nick's injuries were more severe than mine, his losses greater, his future invisible, his strength Herculean, his courage heroic, his spirit indomitable.

And Nick Del Buono has survived. He has done more than that...he has succeeded. Nick Del Buono was severely beaten about the head by a person whose concept of success was very different from his own. Nick Del Buono never boasts of the money he has made nor that he'll make next year, nor of the cachet of his new sports car, nor conquests he's made, how clever he was in closing that latest deal, how beautiful, intelligent, or successful his children are. Why? Because Nick Del Buono has no job, he doesn't play the market, he has no car, the conquests he's made would not be interesting to the "power lunch" crowd, he's closed no deals, and sadly, he has no children.

But Nick Del Buono is an extremely successful man. He has beaten his beater, he is loved by all and hated by no man and he has created life. Money means nothing to him, nor does power; he has created life by enhancing beyond any reasonable expectations my life and the lives of all others who have known him.

Does Nick Del Buono hate his oppressor? I doubt it. Nick has no time for such un-Christian nonsense. You see, Nick Del Buono was severely beaten about the head by a person whose concept of manhood is greatly different from his own. He is busy coping with the vagaries life has thrust upon him and focusing on his assigned mission: *to inspire*. No braggadocio, Nick Del Buono doesn't remind you, even subtly, of his accomplishments.

He leads from strength of character. By dealing for more than twenty years with challenges that would have brought most of us to our knees, *he inspires*.

Our lives are defined by our impact on others. Using this criterion, Nick Del Buono has made his parents, siblings, doctors, caregivers, and me better able to cope with the vagaries of our lives...don't despair for Nick Del Buono. Nick Del Buono has been acknowledged a man, not an invalid. In fact, he may be the most successful man I know.

Dr. Alan Chatt

12

Dr. Stephen Sarfaty

Dr. Stephen Sarfaty is a neuropsychologist in private practice. I met him when John and I became active participants in the movement to get better care for the TBI population in our State of Connecticut. At that time he was associated with the renowned Gaylord Rehabilitation Hospital in Wallingford.

Dr. Sarfaty was and is a very personable man who exudes confidence and spirit. Through many years we have had the pleasure of meeting time and time again as we both share the desire to make things better for all of the young people who are injured and lose the lives they have known to the devastation TBI brings on. We have shared the microphone on several radio shows and worked diligently for the Connecticut Traumatic Brain Injury Association.

My affection for Steve is genuine and long standing. He has been there for me in times of great stress and I appreciate his desire to make his feelings known about Nick.

Dr. Sarfaty's story about Nick

Nicholas Del Buono and I were the same age. We met in 1983 when we were 32 years old. Our lives had taken very different courses. Our meeting gave us an opportunity to be a contribution to each other. Nick is no longer with us to attest to any contribution I may have made to him. I am blessed to be able to testify to the substantial contribution that this wonderful man, Nicholas Del Buono, was, and is, to me.

I first met Nick on March 17, 1983, as a young doctor eager to help but anxious with uncertainty about both my limitations and capabilities. Nick was lying in a nursing home hospital bed at six years and eight and one-half months post serious brain injury acquired during a vicious assault with a baseball bat. The crushing blows, which fractured bones in his face and head, transmitted sufficient force to cause multiple bleeds in and around his brain and destruction of both individual brain cells and brain systems upon which we all rely and take for granted in our daily rounds.

His severe brain injuries were complicated by infections, multiple invasive surgical and life-saving procedures, and years of total nursing care. This torturous course brought him to the day of our first meeting, blind—uncommunicative—and nearly unresponsive, in a nursing home whose odor and atmosphere was more suited to the end of life than any possibility of hope, vitality and relatedness.

It was only just becoming clear, after all the years that passed, that Nick was in fact blind as a consequence of all his injuries. Imagine all the attempts in vain to stimulate him and evaluate him by presenting people and objects to his lifeless visual system. He had already been diagnosed with a seizure disorder whose management remained a substantial obstacle for many years.

His neuropsychological impairments encompassed virtually all of his major brain systems. His limbs were in various states of disordered motor capability, rendering him essentially immobile. Not only was his visual system nonfunctional but detailed understanding of his hearing was complicated by a devastating combination of impairments to his Language Systems and the Oral musculature necessary to support speech. When I first met Nick, he was barely there.

As a young neuropsychologist in my first professional position at the brain injury rehabilitation program at Gaylord Hospital, I had the opportunity to cross paths with Nick's parents, John and Barbara. Along with other parents of brain injured sons and daughters they were urgently advocating with state agencies for the improved care of their family members.

My boss at the time, Dr. Jack Plummer, supported my interest and efforts in responding to requests to represent the rehabilitation professionals' point of view as a partner in these advocacy efforts. John and Barbara represented the epitome of courage, dedication, and persistence seen in so many of the family members of seriously brain injured individuals. It was at their request that I came to be at Nick's bedside and begin a relationship with him that lasted twenty years—and with his parents and family which continues till today.

Good judgment and space do not permit a detailed recounting, not only of the nature of all of Nick's injuries, but also of our shared path in fighting with those injuries and joining with other dedicated individuals in the direct care of brain injured persons and their families, the support of professional care givers, the activities of the interdepartmental committee on brain injury of the State of Connecticut, the founding of the CT Traumatic Brain Injury Support Group and its continuing development, the Governor's Task Force on Traumatic Brain Injury and the day-to-day journey of handling these opportunities in the course of both the mundane and wonderful realities of daily life.

Nick, Steve Sarfaty, Barbara, BIAC Secretary and John

John and Barbara Del Buono are the 1993 recipients of the BIAC Presidents Award

The details of Nick's recovery and his family's efforts toward that end need not be repeated here as they were so wonderfully and completely chronicled in Barbara's book, 'Acknowledged A Man' but suffice it to say that with great risk and effort the family negotiated the combined obstacles of Nick's injury and care, the legal system and the healthcare system and ultimately produced what was essentially a one person rehabilitation center in their home staffed by a loving team of family and professionals who brought Nick to a level of vitality and life which defied every expectation and my highest hopes from the day we first met and I evaluated him in the nursing home bed.

Our paths crossed repeatedly through this journey which was characterized by a combination of repeated evaluations and neuropsychological rehabilitative interventions for Nick.

In the course of family meetings and consultations with various combinations of this wonderful extended family, mundane and epic endeavors and accomplishments were made.

Again, as our paths crossed as board members and support group leaders for the Brain Injury Association, many improved changes were made for the improved care of the brain-injured people of our state. And then our journey resulted in our simply becoming friends while gathered at family weddings, memorials and casual home visits.

Like Jacob, Nick also literally wrestled with devils and angels, (a story in and of itself for another time and place), and through his example my professional work and life was enriched.

Nick's progress and the quality of his life, despite the severity of his acquired limitations from brain injury, destroyed our collective notions of maximal medical improvement. (Italics mine)

As Nick learned to communicate he was a shining example of the power of faith. His shared struggle, with the help of family and caring friends, was an on-going epic leading to victory.

His warmth and generosity to virtually everyone defied our fears and uncertainties about the potential barriers of his disability and taught us the richness of diversity and simple human acceptance. This acceptance, which he shared without qualification, touched, moved and inspired many, including some who had very limited contact with him. Nicholas was a man who lifted us all up as an example of the greatness in ourselves as he challenged us individually and personally to be all that we could be.

I thank God; I thank Nicholas' family; and I thank Nick for being a contribution to me by causing me to exceed my limits. Truly "A Man", and ultimately, a friend!

(Barbara—Reviewing Nick's file was an emotional and informative retrospective. It gave me an opportunity to remember the reason I do what I do and for that I thank you. I acknowledge you and John and your family for all you did for Nick, the many people he touched and the wider community of survivors and their families.

Sincerely yours,
Stephen D. Sarfaty.)"

I italicized one sentence in Dr. Sarfaty's letter because it says so completely what I hoped would be accomplished with the home rehabilitation we were able to help Nick achieve. *"Nick's progress and the quality of his life, despite the severity of his acquired limitations from brain injury, destroyed our collective notions of maximal medical improvement."*

With Nick's rehabilitation I wanted to prove to others that there are no limits to what brain-injury individuals can accomplish if given the opportunity to do so. One thing I know for sure, recovery from brain-injury requires the lives of many people to be successful. But given the sacrifice of these lives, brain-injury persons can be such a catalyst for good in the lives of their care-givers that the sacrifice is well worth the effort. Nick proved that to us everyday of his life. May his marvelous life prove it to others too.

13

Dr. Stephen Rubenstein

Nick's primary-care physician, Dr. Stephen Rubenstein, sent the following sympathy note:

Dear Mr. & Mrs. Del Buono

Please accept my deepest condolences with the death of your son Nick. Although I was only involved with Nick's care at the end of his journey, your loving devotion to him was immediately and considerably obvious to me.

You allowed him to maximize his abilities over these difficult years and I believe he lived longer as a result of your efforts.

I recognize that his passing will create an immense void for you but you should take comfort knowing that although *death may conquer life — it cannot vanquish love.* (Italics mine)

If I can be of help to you during this difficult time, please do not hesitate to call.

Sincerely,

Stephen Rubenstein

Sometimes a thought, a word, or a phrase, has the power to make an immense impression. After Nick's death, when I was so at a loss for words to express the emptiness I felt because he was no longer with us, Dr. Rubenstein's note with the phrase, *"death may conquer life—it cannot vanquish love"* expressed so well what I was feeling.

The love between Nick and me will never end. He may be in heaven and I on earth but love transcends that great divide. I feel his love and I know he feels mine.

14

Sandra Parsons, Private Investigator

Sandra Parsons (Hultman) and her husband, Paul, are very dear friends of ours and have been for many years. Sandra is a very beautiful woman who is a very experienced and competent private investigator. She works with my husband on many of his cases, but I am honored to call her one of my dearest friends. Sandra's personal story about Nick shows the depth of her feelings about him.

This is Sandra's story:

I am a licensed private investigator. When I was first introduced to Nick Del Buono, several years ago, I realized he had been the victim of a malicious assault, severely injured with irreparable brain damage. The injuries extended to the loss of his sight and speech.

It was difficult to know how he interpreted the first hello from me. Suddenly, he brought my hand to his lips and kissed my hand in the manner of a true prince kissing the hand of a lady. I am convinced he understood his mother Barbara's explanation to him of who I was.

In addition to a professional relationship with Nick's parents Barbara and John, I considered them my friends. I could feel the trust he placed in Barbara as I stood along side of her.

"A Man" To Remember

My husband, Paul Hultman, is an artist and created the cover of Barbara Del Buono's first book about Nick, *Acknowledged A Man.* As I got to know Nick a little better, especially after reading *Acknowledged A Man,* I grew interested in what senses he would be able to appreciate and decided it was touch. The kiss on my hand had been a gesture of touch.

When a holiday arrived, I made Nick a blanket. I knew he would never see the horses I sewed into it, but knew it would touch him and keep him warm. I often gave him something soft, like a stuffed animal to touch.

When the world lost Nick to Heaven, I went to his service and took a rose home in remembrance of Nick. The rose died in the hot sun on my dashboard and I thought I would just let it continue dying out and keep the petals.

After arriving home I placed it in a glass of water. I don't really know why. Within a very short time the rose became radiant with color and life. It continued for nearly three weeks, the longest period I have ever seen a rose stay so fresh. Especially one we thought had died. Like Nick, the rose hadn't died at all, and was sending a message of love and thanks from Heaven.

I will always remember Nick with warmth and love.

Sandra Parsons, LPI

15

Paul Hultman, Artist

Paul Hultman is a friend and extraordinary artist. He is known in the art world for his unique variability of style and his diversified themes that include book covers, greeting cards, calendars and paper products. He has also been commissioned to paint murals for corporations and paintings for personal collections. He has had his cartoons and his caricature artwork published. His artwork is international in design as he has his work displayed in children's books, greeting cards and stationery in countries such as Austria, Germany, Pakistan, Switzerland, New Zealand, Norway, the Philippines and the Netherlands.

We felt honored to have Paul paint the picture that is the front and back cover of the book about Nick, *Acknowledged A Man*. What is more of an honor is to be able to call him "friend."

This is Paul's story about Nick:

My most memorable experience with Nick.

Although I had already known Nick for at least 10 years, I believe we responded to each other the most when I was asked by Barbara to illustrate the cover of *Acknowledged A Man*.

I was at their house in the evening during the month of May going over details with Barbara about the design for the cover. After getting a vivid image in my mind concerning the three-headed dragon and the

"A Man" To Remember

symbols, we discussed the image of Nick as being the focal point of the cover.

I asked Barbara if she had photographs that I could reference from and she had quite a few very good pictures to choose from. After studying all of them, and eliminating most of them, I was most impressed with the picture of Nick wearing a white Fedora hat with his arms together. The body language and the angle shot of his face looked perfect for the book. He was relaxed and confident looking. His eyes were toward the camera when the picture was taken.

As we sat discussing various ideas about imposing the design of Nick's image for the cover, I could not help thinking there was something missing from the photo. I wasn't sure what it was that I didn't see that I wanted to see. I was afraid it would also be missing from the completed painting for the book cover and I didn't want that to happen.

I asked John if we could go down to Nick's apartment and visit him for a short while. My thoughts were that if I could get a really good look at Nick while we were talking to him I might be able to find what I was looking for.

John, being a gentleman, greeted Nick in a very mild, polite way. Nick was sitting in a chair listening to John's voice, knowing, but not seeing that he was there. John told Nick that I was there too. Nick put out his hand and I extended mine and we shook briefly.

I asked Nick how he was doing and he smiled for a second but sat completely still. I studied Nick's face while I was standing there. I looked for the missing part I searched for in my mind that would make the image complete. I heard John tell Nick that I was there to see him so that I could study his handsome face for a painting I was going to do of him.

Nick heard that. In fact, he sat up a little and I saw an almost arrogant, but proud look come over him. He smiled again, but this time he had more of a glow. The look in his eyes even changed with that glow. He was being a ham about it. John noticed it too and we both chuckled a little over that.

Well, that glow was the missing part I was looking for and I made it a point to put that glow in the painting. When viewing the book cover, Nick's image is at the center of the dragon heads with a gleam in both eyes and a glow around him. It was the spirit within him that made him glow that evening—the same way I'm sure that he glows now.

Paul Hultman

16

Ann Sheldon, School Teacher

Ann Sheldon is a dear friend to John and me. When she was a nun with the Daughters of Wisdom, she taught four of our children at Mt. Carmel School. We have remained good friends over all these years. She has been with us in good times and in bad. She left the convent and is now a retired English teacher.

Nick met her at the convent when he was just a teenage boy. She answered the doorbell and he exclaimed that if she was the bride of Christ, he sure did envy Him. She is a beautiful woman.

Inspiration

*I remember a man almost devoid of life
laying in a hospital bed.
(how fragile the human frame)*

*I saw this man struggle beyond his limitations:
no sight, yet he saw who was there,
legs weak and maimed, yet in time, he walked;
brain damaged, yet he talked with me.
I felt wonder.*

*In the environs of love, he birthed again.
A new man strong in Spirit, living faith,
I felt courage – more than courage,
hope and love.*

Nicky, thank you!

17

Deborah Del Buono, Sister

Nick's sister, Debbie, was ten years younger in age than he, but not in spirit. They understood each other and had a unique relationship. Debbie was still in high school when Nick was injured and it was almost as traumatic for her as for Nick. It certainly changed both lives dramatically.

Nick, as well as all his family, would have had a different kind of life if this tragedy had not happened but I think that, most of all, Debbie would have had a better one. Nick had the ability to influence Debbie's life and though she remained as close to him as she could, what could have been has always haunted her.

These are Debbie's thoughts about Nick:

Nick, your life and death has made me dream of a life after death—and that is a very important gift for someone like me who is so easily prone to believe otherwise.

I never really could understand how you embraced losing your physical abilities the way you did. I have tried hard to live my life the way you wanted me to. Since you were injured I have had a difficult time doing it. If it weren't for you and Mom and Dad helping me, I would not have been able to do as much as I have. The three of you taught me to learn how to find a way to come around and embrace what happened by forgiveness which you, my kindred spirit,

"A Man" To Remember

were so capable of and willing to do. "Learn to love thy enemy." This is a hard lesson to learn in life. I will clearly spend the years ahead focusing on this lesson based on what has happened since that fateful day. I know that you will be my guide in this endeavor.

Nick, when you took me to see the ping pong players, the pool hall, the *King Kong* movie, to the discos, and the *Death of A Salesman* play, I began to believe that it was possible to find something to do with my life that I really enjoy and get paid for it too. Though I haven't completely realized that dream yet, I will keep trying.

We had big dreams of doing things together, Nick, but instead we were limited to my reading books to you, walking with you in your walking bar and going to concerts once in a while. You made the holidays bearable for me as we would sit and read while Mom fixed holiday dinners.

We both had set-backs in our lives and when we fell down together, I would try to break the fall and you would always guide us upwards. Each step was an incredible time step. I can't wait to dance in Heaven with ya Nick. I know that I will be that quick study of yours when I get there.

The most important dream of all though has been realized—having a beautiful girl and boy and creating a loving family—a brother and sister. I am so glad they are named after you my dear brother. They will inherently carry your beautiful spirit and will transmit its meaning without saying words because like you used

"A Man" To Remember

to say, "talk is cheap."

The letters that you wrote to me when you were in the Air Force gave me a desire to dream big and to do something good with my life. I know that you are proud of me because I have managed pretty well. I finished college and got my Master's Degree and have worked at one job for the last ten years. I could not have done all of this without your help. I will now try to do something different.

I miss you and need you to sometimes take my mixed up words and blow down a special brand of your common sense to help me through the rest of my life—as only you can do, because our conversations will never really stop, huh, Nick.

I am reminded sometimes of a distant bell with a barely visible beacon of light—and believe it is you, sending signals to me from far away—since you died. (You really are a sucker for a happy ending, aren't you?) It is like a ham radio signal, I hear it but I can't see it just yet, but I will explore it further until I do. It certainly feels like it is heaven sent.

Thanks for giving me this seventh sense, Nick. I believe it will carry me far through the dreaded darkness when I feel abandonment and know it will never totally sweep me away. I have been truly blessed to have you as my big brother who is now safe up in Heaven. I say to you now what you wrote to me in your last letter from the Air Force.

Now and forever yours,
Deborah Jean

18

Johnny Del Buono, Nephew

There must be a rare gift that is bestowed on men named John Del Buono. I have lived with three of them: John Angelo, my husband, John Nicholas, our son, and John James, our grandson. All three are blessed with so much charm it seems to ooze out of every pore of their skin. Extroverts all—and more, as they bring joy to life and make you feel important just being around them. They are full of love and kindness but can be impish in the flash of a second.

Our grandson, Johnny, is seventeen years old now. He spent a great deal of time with his Uncle Nick as a young boy and learned to love him very much. They played games together and *Yahtzee* was a favorite because Nick could shake the dice and have someone add up his score. He often won the game. They often listened to movies together and always enjoyed each other's taste in music.

Johnny was another one of those rare individuals who did not seem to grasp the fact that Nick was extremely handicapped. He treated him as normal and Nick treated Johnny the same way.

"A Man" To Remember

At times Johnny could be quite a handful as a young lad. Once when Nick was sitting in his swing chair in the family room, Johnny was coming out with quite a bit of sass and Nick didn't like it. He reached out his left hand to grab Johnny but couldn't quite reach him. He told Mary, "You hold him, and I'll spank him." Mary didn't follow through on that command but it did put some fear in Johnny as to what his uncle would do to him if he continued to talk like that.

This is Johnny's statement about his Uncle Nick:

To me, Nick is a role-model for role-models. You see movies about super heroes that conquer evil and save the people. My Uncle Nick definitely defeated evil every day of his life and has been such an impact on other people's lives—and my own life. I can surely say he is a super uncle.

Johnny writes songs and he wrote one for his Uncle Nick. The lyrics go like this:

> I wish they had a prescription for your disease
> because it's getting harder to breathe.
>
> When everybody's saying drop,
> but no, your body doesn't stop.
>
> You live.
>
> I think this life has got to learn to give
> because you give all of your love free of debt.

"A Man" To Remember

This man's a machine dated 1951

But he doesn't need any gasoline
Pumping on adrenalin
Speeding up with passion.

Yeah, you're probably wondering
how he's lasted this long

But you feel this love
and it gets you higher
The rest are second best
when it comes to the fire
Burning in this man's chest.

And they tried swallowing him whole,
Almost got his body
But never touched his soul.

And if you ask me why
I'd say simply because the man can.

Love you Uncle Nick
Johnny

19

Joan McKnight, Sister

Nick's sister, Joan, lives in California and has been a high school physics teacher in Orange County for many years. She sent him the following card in which she changed the lyrics by substituting Nick's name for Tommy from the Rock Opera, *Tommy*, by *The Who*. It was sent to him shortly after his injury many years ago but it shows how deep her emotions were for Nick.

Nicky Can You Hear Me...

Can You Feel Me Near You...

Nicky Can You See Me...

Can I Help To Cheer You...

Nicky...Nicky...Nicky...Nicky...

How often did we listen to the first Rock Opera together in history?

You seem to permeate my dreams quite often—it seems the dreams are strange but positive. I have come to wonder if part of the dreams aren't being perpetuated by you. Just like a person gone blind—all other senses accentuate; I wonder if your sixth sense steps up in the absence or repair of the other. I'm sure you understand what I mean—you always measured yourself in broad horizons of ideas & possibilities. I see no reason to limit those now.

You may have been told I was back there in the summer. I shall return my friend. It seems that the better you get, the closer the family gets—perhaps one cannot occur without the energy derived from the other. Whatever may be, Nicky, I only know that you seem to exert an influence on the constellation of people that surround you—whether you are able to speak or not.

I may be able to return to the Eastern part of this country next year (perhaps this summer). But when I do, I can think of no better reason to come than to be able to look you in the eye, and say hello, and to maybe have you say hello back, anyway you choose to do so.

Just remember, Nicky, I am always with you—a thought is a wave of energy emitted the same as any other wave—like radio, etc. Much energy is, and has been, sent your way.

I love you Nicky

Joanie

20

Cathy Jewett, Sister

Cathy Jewett is Nick's youngest sister. She has two beautiful sons, Christopher and Jason, both of whom loved their Uncle Nick dearly. They watched (and he listened) to movies together and they were the recipients of his wonderful hugs. When Nick hugged you, you really knew you were loved and these children had the wonderful experience of knowing this. Few uncles give to their nieces and nephews what Uncle Nick gave to his. Cathy's remembrances of her brother are poignant and sweet.

I Remember

The last words spoken
Yet the hardest to reach.
Inspirations fostered
Each moment to teach.

No moments to waste,
No challenge too great.
Take each as they come
And rise above each one.

Nick's last words to me were, "I remember." We spoke of times when I was young and he took me on hikes through the woods, fishing for the first time, how to ride a bike, and how to tie my shoes. I remember too.

He had been through so much and I'd always wondered, "Does he carry these thoughts as I do?"

And then, hours before his new journey began, we spoke, and he lovingly told me, "I remember too."

No greater gift in my life could there be than Nick's inspiration. His spirit so bright and his hope so unending, he inspires us still to reach our own ending. Nick gave us all the stars to reach for. He showed us how and gave us peace.

The sky lit up as his journey began—as if to say, "no worries, be glad." Yet another inspiring memory Nick leaves us all with. As the heavens know, Nick truly is a gift.

I will always remember you, Nick.

Cathy

The most marvelous part of this story is that Nick truly did remember. His long-term memory was not destroyed and we could all talk endlessly with him about the years when he was growing up and our family was all together in a loving home.

As I have told my children often, the greatest part of my life was in nurturing them through childhood into adults. The memories are sweet and very precious, Cathy. I remember too.

21

Sally Houseknecht, Sister

Sally is Nick's younger sister. She and Nick had opposite personalities and thoroughly enjoyed exploring each other's traits—sometimes with arguments. Nick was the out-going extrovert, full of energy and always ready to entertain. Sally was the shy, demure young lady who exuded an air of weakness but when you got close you found a will of iron. The love between these two would have been hard to discern on the surface but test it and you found it very deep and fervent.

This is Sally's story about her brother.

One of my earliest memories of my brother Nick is when I was around 5 years old. I recall going for a walk in the woods with several of my brothers and sisters. We were near the water tower in Murray Park. I recall tripping and I hit my head on a rock. I remember Nick swooping down to pick me up and I remember him running as fast as he could to carry me home.

They say you remember specific things from your childhood that stood out to you for some reason. I know I had a pretty decent bump on my head and my parents took me to the doctor. The emotion I attach to that experience the most, and the reason I think I remember it so vividly, is how much my brother cared for me. It still makes me feel like how nice it was to have a big brother looking out for you.

"A Man" To Remember

Nick was away for years in the military. When he came home we used to go to the basement late at night and talk. I was around 17 years old. We would stay up very late. The most memorable thing that came out of that experience is that I recall Nick was determined to convince me to read this trilogy. He insisted on reading chapters and chapters of the first book out loud to me.

Now you must understand no one can read a book like Nick. He became the characters. I became completely enchanted with the story and then the author. I read them over and over again. It was *The Lord of the Rings*. I remember him speaking like *Gollum* the most. It was better than the movie. I got a lifetime of enjoyment as the Tolkien fan I still am. It all started with Nick.

It was also during this time when Nick was home he had occasion to meet a boyfriend of mine. My parents were not too crazy about me seeing this guy. Nick sat down and talked with him and me when he was around. One day when my boyfriend left, I was in the basement. Nick popped his head down the stairs and simply said, "I think you are more like a mother to him than a girlfriend." I stopped seeing this guy after that.

Nick was a trip. He used to wear a top hat and take his flute—while wearing a black, velvet jacket and he would go for walks in the woods playing his flute. I have never met a more interesting and unique individual. Nick judged everyone and everything for himself. He definitely walked to the beat of his own drum.

On another occasion while Nick was away, he heard that Debbie and I were going through some troubled times. He sent a postcard to us that stands out in my mind. I will never forget what he wrote and I have remembered it many times. It simply said, "There's no way to delay that trouble coming every day. Love, Nick."

Nick came home from California to live at home several months before he was injured. He and I worked together at Dad's law office and shared a home and had to share a vehicle. This was an interesting experience.

No one in my entire life has ever cared to find out what was in my mind and what I believed and knew as much as Nick. He was fascinated with picking my brain and challenging all of my thoughts. He loved sharing his philosophy and discussions of existentialism.

As brother and sister will do, particularly in such close contact every day, we fought some times. I remember being angry with him, and for the first time in my life, and actually the last, I gave him the silent treatment. It had to be for a day or two. I remember being surprised by how much my brother actually cared.

When Nick was assaulted I was home alone when Mom and Dad called. I ran two miles to my brother Joe's house because there was no answer on the phone. I left a note for him and walked home. I didn't know what else to do.

In the months and years to follow, while Nick was in coma, I remember going to the hospital hoping this would be the day he would wake up and everything would be okay. That one day never came. But slowly, gradually, over time, Nick's mind came back. With incredible devotion from Mom and Dad, and the work of caring nurses, doctors and therapists Nick was able to communicate.

The one thing I am quite sure of is that Nick experienced a close encounter of the first kind with God. I believe, without a doubt, that although Nick's horrible trauma was a tragedy of the worst kind, it was, at the same time, the most blessed experience that, as the Bible says, you are a new creature in Christ Jesus.

I remember visiting Nick in the nursing home so many times when he would say, "I see God" or "I see angels" or, at times, demons. The spiritual world is all around us all the time. We co-exist with them without realizing this for most of our lives. I believe Nick's condition allowed him to experience the spiritual world more intensely than the physical world for his remaining life.

Nick was glad to be alive. Nick touched so many lives spiritually—which is more than most people can say. When you go through a difficult time and think, "I can't handle this," stop and remember Nick. In his pure state of being completely in God's grace, you have the most perfect example I have witnessed of how to deal with life's blows.

I have been completely inspired by Nick. He may have had a difficult time expressing what he had to say, but if you took the time to ask, and listen, you heard the most profoundly simple answers that hit right to the heart of the matter. After that you have no question in your mind of Nick's mental state.

I was, at the same time, inspired by the loving devotion of Mom, Dad, Mary, Gail, Deb, Carly and all those who cared for Nick.

    I will always miss my brother. I love you Nick. I know you are in heaven now.

Love, Sally

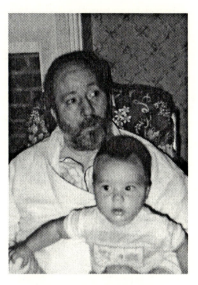

Nick with Sally's son Michael who is Nick's Godson.

22

Peter Casteel, Nephew

Peter Casteel is Mary's oldest child, our first grandchild, and the anticipated baby whose birth Nick celebrated so joyously. He was just a tot, 4 years of age, when his uncle was injured. For a while he remembered his uncle Nick but then the memory of who he was and what he was like before he was injured, faded. But the uncle he remembers is beautifully told.

Remembered: An Uncle

When a loved one dies, there are many feelings that hit you. Some come all at once. Some come later, with time. It's different also whether the person passes spontaneously, or if the person knows he or she is dying; that his or her days on earth are numbered; and that his or her friends and family have the opportunity to share those final moments with them. Such was the case with Nick.

I'll always remember telling my mom that I felt lucky to have the opportunity to visit Nick and to not leave anything unsaid. With that opportunity, I told Nick—no, I *thanked* Nick—for being the person above all others I have ever met to show me what faith is all about.

Not the easiest word to define—faith. It's probably easier to **experience** faith than it is to **describe** faith. No one I ever knew lived every minute

"A Man" To Remember

with more faith than Uncle Nick. Of all the things I admired about him, the one I admired most about my Uncle Nick is...F A I T H.

I remember a time in high school when one of my friends came over and saw a picture of Nick on the wall and he asked: "Whoa! Is that a picture of Jesus Christ?"

I smiled and said, "What would you say if I told you his birthday was December 20—something?"

"No. Really! Is that a real picture? Who is that?"

My friend really thought Nick looked like Jesus.

When I told Nick, he really took it as a compliment. He sure tried to live his life in a Christian way. He was the rare person who would **pray always**—Nick prayed all the time. And he also would **pray all ways**—Nick used every means he could to pray to God. Everything he did, in a sense, could be considered a prayer.

About eight or so years ago, I put a homily I'd recently heard to the test. In this homily, the priest was talking about novenas. (*Latin for "nine."*) In summary, he said that God has made a promise to us through his saints that if you truly pray for something,

Pray with your head
Pray with your lips, and
Pray with your heart.

And, if you say that prayer nine times a day for nine consecutive days, God will grant you anything. Then he warned, "Be careful what you wish for."

Therefore, heeding this advice, I had to word my prayer very carefully, and I also figured I should keep it simple—so that my heart and head and lips could all be true. So I prayed these three words:

"RESTORE NICK'S SIGHT."

Nine times, nine days, I prayed. The tenth day the phone rang. It was my mom. Nick had had some tests done and the doctor calculated that he could perceive a higher percentage of light than they had previously measured.

I was floored! It worked! Sure, I "meant" for him to no longer be blind, but that wasn't exactly what I prayed for now, was it? "Restore Nick's Sight." Just a little. Done. And how did that happen? **Faith.**

Now, could his loss of sight in any way be seen as a blessing in disguise? I have no doubt that he could see angels. No doubt that he developed a second sight. No doubt that he was given a gift of using another sense.

Part of me wonders if this was meant to be. Part of me wonders if it would have happened had he not been blind. Perhaps he's had this gift all of his life, but when looking at the world through his "human" eyes, he wasn't able to distinguish what he was truly "seeing." Do you *see* what I mean? I believe he was granted insights into Heaven. And that he talked to God on a level that I still envy. In fact, I don't have any doubt that Nick is in Heaven right now. Now that is faith!

"A Man" To Remember

One of the great things about loving someone is getting to know and to love those close to them. For instance, I know my relationship with my Grandma and my Grandpa was made ever deeper because we three shared a loving relationship with Nick. And how about my sister-from-another-mister, Nick's namesake Nicole!

Furthermore, it's hard to remember Uncle Nick without also remembering some friendly angels so near to him. As a teacher or leader or caregiver, often one's examples can show more than one's words. Well, words cannot explain how Carly, Debbie and Gail not only enriched Nick's life, but mine as well. Boy, have you truly become an extended family! With six sisters and a brother, Nick's circle of love sure was a wide one after these true friends joined it.

Now I have to say a word about my mom and her relationship with her brother. What word can I use, then? Devotion? Dedication? Caring? Fidelity? Affection? Support? Attentiveness? Ask me for anything and you've got it Mister! Sisterly love? Ah! Now we're getting there. All of the above were there in great supply. But above all these, there's love. If my Uncle Nick showed me how to live faithfully, his sister, my mother, was the one who showed me how to love.

It feels a little weird to be writing about Nick. Not because he's in Heaven now, more so because Grandma's written 350 plus pages (and counting). And still I keep falling back on exactly **one** piece of paper she wrote about him. It still resonates true after 20 plus years. It still sums up what Nick is about in so many ways:

Nick is blind
But he can see straight into your heart
every time you are near him.

Nick cannot speak words
But he will tell you a story about yourself
you never knew.

Nick cannot walk
But he will take a stroll through your life
from the moment you meet him.

Nick is one incredible fellow
You will be glad you met him.

We all know the saying: God prepares a place for us in Heaven. I believe Nick was a help in preparing **his** place. I believe Nick is where he so often wanted to go. I believe that for many years God shared Nick with us so he could continue to bless us. I believe Nick is exactly where he belongs. And I believe that he's there now helping to prepare special places for each of us.

>So, until I see you again…
>Praise you and thank you Uncle Nick!
>Your loving nephew, Peter

23

Amy Dean, Niece

Amy Dean is Nick's niece, Mary's daughter. She grew up visiting Nick in nursing homes and charming all the patients with her sweet smile and pleasant attitude. She is grown up now, married and the mother of five beautiful children.

She has always been comfortable in Nick's presence and has brought a great deal of joy to him whether injured or not. When he arrived back in Connecticut from California, we met him at the airport and Amy was in the car. She was so intrigued by him that she stood on the axel hump in the back seat and talked to him incessantly. No one else could get a word with him.

Nick played with Amy through all of her *Cabbage Patch* doll days and enjoyed her little girl games. He was newly injured when she was growing up and could not interact with her and her brother Peter the way he did later with many of his nieces and nephews.

Amy's letter to Nick:

Dear Uncle Nicky,

I wanted to thank you for all the things you have taught me through the example of your life. The two things that stand out most in my mind are *love* and *contentment*.

"A Man" To Remember

By love, I mean the love you had for every person in your family. From the smallest baby bouncing on your lap, the young kids that made you smile as you heard them playing, the teenagers you faithfully prayed for, to the adults that you gave wonderful advice to.

You also taught me about love for life. To cherish the simple blessings, like the songs of a bird and the warmth of the sun. I pray that I can always remember to appreciate the little things in life and not be overwhelmed by the daily stresses.

Most importantly you taught me about love for our Lord Jesus. Others may have become bitter if put in your place. But you reminded me of the importance of prayer, and to remember that there is an unseen spiritual battle going on all around us. We need to be sure we're following and pleasing the Lord each day.

The Bible says whatsoever state we're in to be content. This is a lot easier said than done, except with you. I would like to think that whatever tragedies come into my life, I'd be able to humbly accept it, and continue to praise God as you have. You never complained about your circumstances, just thanked God for each new day. This is an important lesson that we would all do well to learn from.

It used to bother me that I didn't know you before you were hurt, but I realize now that the Uncle Nicky I had was the best there is. I look forward to seeing you again. Thanks for everything.

Love,
Amy

"A Man" To Remember

There is a poem by Lois Parrish that Amy draws comfort from and wishes to share:

We'll See Them Again

The sun has gone to rest beneath the lake,
And one by one the little stars awake,
But do not think because it slips from view,
The sun has bid the earth a last adieu.
We say the sun has come to rest when night
Drops a veil that dims the mortal sight;
But it has risen on another world,
The petals of its golden bloom unfurled,
And there the robin in the treetop sings,
And warmth and light awake all waiting things.

And so "at rest" is what we sometimes say
Of that dear one who gently slipped away;
But he has simply vanished from the earth
To find elsewhere a new and glorious birth;
Lost to our sight a little tearful while,
His tender voice, his quick and eager smile.
But surely as the faithful, rising sun
Returns to bless our eyes, so will this one
Be waiting when the dawn of dawns appears,
So put away your sorrow and your tears,
And know that you will see him face to face,
Whose light already shines in that far place.

24

Kyle Houseknecht, Nephew

Kyle Houseknecht is Nick's nephew, his sister Sally's son. In the early years of his life he spent many days with Nick as Mary and I baby-sat with him while his mother worked. He had a very special relationship with Nick and played games with him, even as a four-year-old child. One that Nick thoroughly enjoyed was when Kyle would make sounds of different animals and then Nick would have to guess what animal it was. They both loved this game.

As Kyle grew into a young teenager (he is fifteen years old now), he became an excellent baseball player and a star pitcher. Nick never got to see him play but he heard many times about the great Kyle on the baseball field pitching winning games and occasionally a no-hitter. Kyle's insights about Nick are very precious.

Kyle's story about Nick

You always hear about the great American heroes that inspire millions and become examples for the future generations to marvel about. But what makes them a hero? Could they be the tragic heroes of 9/11 who gave their lives to save the remainder of survivors and search relentlessly for family members? Are they the great legends of baseball like Mickey Mantle, playing despite being hurt; Don Mattingly, with his bad back for most of his career; or even the Iron Horse, Lou Gehrig? All of them suffered on the field, but were phenomenal. Yet all of these famous names are remembered most for the way they were off the field, how they were as a person.

The gallant man I knew that shadows over all feats of strength and defied all odds would not accept that there was no chance of hope. A man who had so much potential for a great person at whatever he would have chosen to pursue, but this shimmer of God's light was muffled for a brief time.

John Nicholas Del Buono is this hero who has an untold story to parallel any of the great ones who preceded him. He was a man who could not see; could hardly walk; who would need to learn a new language to communicate. He was the worst example of a tamed spirit, yet born to be free and gallant, a unicorn among mustangs is what Nick was.

He was a God-fearing man who had a large influence over hundreds who knew him personally, and then thousands who heard his story. Over the years, after his attack, Nick was able to walk again; able to see shadows and colors; and also had gained a great, constant supporting system that gave him a loving and nurturing home.

Nick said he had talked to angels and it would seem true from how blessed he was. No one could be envious of him, but happy that some one so deserving was able to experience something so precious as God's messengers speaking to you.

It must have been God's choice for Nick to see only the purest of pure, and he deserved to see them. From having to look death in the face he must have made God want Nick to see the great instead of the horrid.

The beginning and end to this story are not happy, but melancholy, because he is no longer here to light up the room he's in. But we know now that where he has gone is a constant, supreme happiness that is infinite. So seeing Nick in heaven, flawless, like his spirit was on earth, will make being in heaven even greater because he will be happy.

Kyle Houseknecht.

25

Christina Greenway, Cousin

Christina Greenway is my brother's middle child. She is my dear niece who I got to know only for a short time when she was a child. Due to divorce, we lost track of each other for many years and then one beautiful day she came back into my life. She never got to meet Nick but his life touched hers deeply through the many letters we wrote back and forth, the phone calls, and finally through the book that I wrote about him.

Christina sent Nick this poem by Helen Steiner Rice one year just before Christmas. It is another one that appropriately applies to Nick's life. He enjoyed it very much and I read it to him many times.

The Legend of the Wingless Bird

"Oh for the wings of a bird," he cries
To carry me off to an untroubled sky,
Where I can dwell untouched by care,
And always be free as a bird in the air.

But there is a legend that is very old
Not often heard and seldom told,
That once all birds were wingless, too,
Unable to soar through the skies of blue—

For while their plumage was beautifully bright
And their chirping songs were liltingly light,
They too were powerless to fly
Until one day when the Lord came by
And laid at the feet of the singing birds
Gossamer wings as He spoke these words,

"Come, take these burdens so heavy now,
But if you bear them you'll learn somehow
That as you wear them they will grow light,
And soon you can lift yourself in flight."

So folding the wings beneath their hearts,
And after endless failures and starts,
They lifted themselves and found with delight
The wings that were heavy had grown so light.

So let me, too, listen to God's wise words,
For I am much like the wingless bird,
And if I shoulder all my daily trials,
And learn to wear them with sunny smiles,
I will find the wings that God has sent
To lift me above my heart's discontent.

For the wings that lift me out of despair
Are made by God from the weight of care,
So whenever I cry for the wings of a bird,
I remember this little legend that you have heard
And I let God give me a heart that sings
As he turns my daily burdens into silver wings."

"A Man" To Remember

Christina wrote the following poem herself in honor of Nick.

To My Cousin Nick

Each and every day
for the past two and a half years,
healing from my thyroid surgery,
I have felt his love of God,
Love of Life,
And his Love for all fellow man,
And I gained new strength daily
As I heard Nick say
Across all the miles between us,

"My cross is not too heavy,
My road is not too rough,
Because my God walks beside me
And to know that is enough."

One thing I have learned from the strength,
Character, and Love of God
Is that all who do meet him
I am sure feel the same as I do
That "on Life's busy thoroughfare,
Once in a lifetime
we all will meet Angels Unaware."

I hope and pray daily that Nick's siblings
Are not too busy to listen
Or too busy to sense that God is near,
And may silently ask themselves,

"If I was this wingless bird
that Nick is now
Who reaches out so gently
to touch our lives daily,

"A Man" To Remember

Do I realize how lucky I am that
There but for the Grace of God I could be?"

Could I be the Angel that Nick is,
To all the lives he daily touches?
Words cannot express the bountiful gifts
Of strength, Courage and Love of God,
That I have learned from my cousin Nick.

To know him is to know Phoenix Rising
And to be called his friend in Life
Is truly an honor.

His cousin
Christina Greenway

After Nick's death Christina wrote the following and sent it to me.

God's Master Plan For Nick

In God's Master Plan Nick was sent to us as a beautiful rose, and we thank God for the years we had with him.

He lived his life well, Lord, and has seen the cycle of life and death, and he will be missed. He touched so many lives in such a special way Lord, and we all learned so much of God's love from him.

As we mourn the loss of him here, Nick has now gained his wings in heaven. His life on earth reminds me of a "crushed rose" in the Garden of God.

In life I never knew Nick, yet, somehow, one day I strayed along a pathway, where God's idle fancy led me on a well-worn path beside a hedge, where God's Garden of Roses bloomed ever so free.

I stooped to breathe in the perfumed air, but paused. At my feet lay a beautiful rose, crushed and bruised, that once had been Nick, so fair and sweet.

I gently lifted the crushed rose, and wondered at the careless foot that trod so heavily to make Nick's path so steep and hard in life. When lo! I began to breathe in the sweet fragrance of the rose and the aroma seemed to rise to Heaven and touch the throne of God.

Nick was our trampled rose in life; a bruised soul that God only let us have for such a short while. Nick taught us much in his short life. When he was crushed beneath life's terrible strife, he taught us never to quit or blame God—and never to stop loving Him.

He is gone from us now, yet, somehow, the sweet smell of Nick's life as a crushed rose in the Garden of God remains with us still. We thank God for this beautiful gift of a man He sent us from Heaven.

Amen.

"A Man" To Remember

26

Judie Gunn, Cousin

Judie Gunn is another one of Nick's cousins and the daughter of my dear sister Ann who lived in Albuquerque, New Mexico. Ann died just two years before Nick and she made more than one trip east to see her dear nephew. On one occasion Judie accompanied her so she had the opportunity to meet Nick. Immediately after hearing of Nick's death, Judie wrote the following beautiful poem for Nick.

The Gift

By Judie Gunn

In memory of Nick Del Buono

There was a young man...
Whose destiny was unknown...
He was young and vibrant...
As his seeds were being sown...

"A Man" To Remember

He laughed and danced
with good cheer and joy…
He was a man,
with the heart of a boy…

That fateful day…
When all was thought lost…
Thru hate and envy…
With a heavy cost…

The young man's seeds
that had been sown…
Were scattered by the wind…
To places unknown…

Through heartache and pain…
Thru so much despair…
This young man
had something to share…

He taught all to LOVE,
to FORGIVE and LIVE…
That's what GOD
said he would give…

Nick had a purpose
while he was here…
To teach us that GOD
is always near…

To look in his eyes
full of awesome GRACE…
Is to see GOD
In his beautiful face…

"A Man" To Remember

GOD took him home
and set him free...
Now he soars
and can finally see!

He LIVES again
in an awesome place...
With wide open fields
and lots of space...

He sees those who LOVE him...
Both here and THERE...
He lives again
without a care...

His FAMILY, GOD given,
Held steadfast and strong...
Gave him a life
full of praise and song...

What a wonderful blessing
GOD gave to you...
Now with HIS GRACE,
HE will see you thru...

You'll hear those words
"JOB WELL DONE"...
The great reward
that is to come...

27

Ted Phipps, TBI Caregiver

There is a website for care-givers of the brain injured population of the *world*. To access this website you must be caring for a brain-injured person. Stories, strategies, new technology, and the most important thing of all, comfort, is shared and the knowledge that you are not alone in your isolated world.

Our daughter, Mary, belongs to this group and while she has met many wonderful people whose stories she has shared with me, one person is outstanding and I would like to share some of his story. His name is Ted Phipps and he lives in England. He too has a blind TBI son. He is truly a remarkable man.

On July 26, 2004, he sent Mary an e-mail letter:

Hello Mary,

Having just finished reading your Mum's book I feel I must write to you to say just how much I appreciated it and how enthralled I was to follow the history of Nick's tragedy and the way your parents, you, and the rest of your family, dealt with all the consequences of that vicious attack.

Of all the people who have read that book only those in a similar situation can really empathize with many of the aspects that she covered and the pain that you all went through.

The problems brought on by Nick's blindness

were so similar to those we experienced. In fact there are so many similarities in both our loved ones problems that I cannot say I have ever met anyone else in the TBI world to whom I can relate in a similar fashion.

The thing that amazed me was how your Mum was able to recall such detail and feelings of emotion after such a long time. Someone must have kept a remarkable diary of events and recorded every day.

In our case I think time has now faded memories of many of our experiences and names of the many medics and hospital workers etc are now lost in the mists of time. Your Mum's book certainly helped to recall some of our experiences again and I relived many of the painful times once more (not that it has quite the same impact nowadays. Perhaps our trauma with the loss of our other son Andrew after his two year battle with Non Hodgkin's Lymphoma since then has mollified that).

In Andrew's case there were so many of his friends and relatives who wanted to know of his progress but were too reluctant to keep calling us that I issued detailed bulletins at periodic intervals and distributed them. Someone suggested that I keep them to remind the younger members of the family in later life the trauma that we were going through.

I did just that and now on a reread it reminds me of much of your book albeit not nearly so long, not so detailed and certainly not so eloquently written. Pam, my wife, reread it recently and it reduced her to tears once more. I wonder if rereading your book now that Nick is no longer around will have the same effect on your family.

I can only hold the greatest admiration for your Mother's stamina and dogged determination to do the best for Nick and to your father too for the tireless effort he put in on the legal side. I guess being a lawyer was a great asset in the legal battle with the YMCA.

I found the comparison between your American legal system and our English system very interesting. Julie, our daughter, was a solicitor at that time and took up Ian's legal battle for him together with the other lawyers in her firm. At times though her assistance brought more work for me! "You can sort out that problem for me Dad—can't you?—whilst I get on with some of the others!"

The English legal system is much more formal; for example solicitors can only speak to senior council QC's (Queen's councilors) through the junior council (barrister) and the only way the plaintiff can approach the law is through the solicitor representing him. In the High Court, where damages are usually settled, only QC's are allowed to hold discussions with the Judge.

When we attended Court everything was going on so far above our heads as though we were not even there. Selection of the right QC to represent you is of the utmost importance if you are to have a successful outcome. Fortunately in our case we had a successful outcome and it hit the National TV News Bulletins as one of the highest awards at that time in Britain. Before we had left the Royal Courts of Justice in London, the TV companies were on our doorstep as we reached home!

I greatly admire too, Mary, your devotion to Nick as a much loved brother and the enormous amount of effort you put in over the years to assist in the remarkable recovery he made. Bringing up a young family and looking after your husband at the same time could not have been easy.

Now that Nick's life has come to an end I wonder how you are all coping without him and how, having been relieved of the care and rehabilitation aspect of it all, you are managing to rebuild your lives. I am also sure that knowing it was entirely due to your family efforts that Nick was able to make such a remarkable recovery and to enjoy so many years of extra life is now a great comfort to you.

Both the older and younger members of your family have fulfilled a role that will hold you all in good stead for the rest of your lives. Nick will live on in memory and remain a shining example of courage and fortitude in the face of such overwhelming obstacles and problems.

Given the opportunity I will read sections of the book to Ian but my wife and Paul, Ian's carer, are first in queue to read the book and then perhaps I may loan it to our TBI day centre 'Headway' where many of the staff would be very interested in reading about your experiences.

Many thanks again for Nick's tapes which will be played in due course to Ian. Maybe the American accents will be a novelty to him although we get so many American TV programs these days that perhaps it won't make that much difference and he will certainly be able to follow the dialogue.

We are looking forward now to another cruise shortly taking Ian and another helper with us. Unfortunately nowadays my wife is classified as being disabled herself and she can only travel if an able-bodied person accompanies her. I do not qualify as I am officially Ian's carer. This time we are traveling south to Spain, Portugal and the Atlantic Canary Islands and Madeira. Fourteen nights and cloudless skies (hopefully).

Ian, like Nick, loves to walk and the promenade deck on a cruise liner is ideal as there is a hand rail virtually all around the ship. He can walk unaided, enjoying the sun and sea air with me trailing behind in his wheelchair telling him to avoid the lifebelt and to stop before he walks into the lifeboat. It becomes a daily ritual for us. We are all looking forward to the break (Especially me—No cooking!)

Once again Mary many thanks for thinking of Ian and thank both you and your family for sharing your book with us. I am sure all the brain injured of America hold you all in gratitude for your contribution to the progress made in improving the care of this unfortunate group of people.

Take care, enjoy your loving family and remember the good times had with Nick—I am sure he dwells on that from above too!

> Ted, Pam and Ian who hold you and your family in our prayers.

28

Jacqueline Daddona, Nurse

Nurses were often very affected by Nick and his attitude toward the kind of life he had to live. Many of them were complimentary about the skin care he received and were always impressed with Nick's attitude about himself, his injury and his faith.

Mary D'Agata was one at the beginning of his journey. Jacqueline Daddona was one during his last hospital stay.

At the end of his life we received the following sympathy card from her. She designed the card and took her valuable time to send it to us. How very pleased we were to get it.

The one you love
Will live on forever

With Deepest Sympathy

Many patients come through my life, few make a lasting impression. Nick was one of those who not only touched my heart but inspired me to take my sense of compassion to

A higher level.

I'm deeply saddened by his loss. My prayers are with you and your family in this very difficult time.

Sincerely,

Jacqueline Daddona R N
Pomeroy 7

29

Death Cannot Vanquish Love

This is a book about love that had to be written. It is about the triumph of one man over the unimaginable tragedy of a criminal assault. I felt compelled to write it after Nick's death. The depth of love that this man inspired is so extraordinary that it defines the word "love" and makes it live. I hope that is apparent in the stories and tributes paid to him.

Nick was so injured that he was deprived of the ordinary means of showing his love but he managed to do it in ways that touched all of us deeply. In return we could not help but love him back. We were more than compensated for any perceived sacrifices we made. He proved with his life after injury that a so-called "fate worse than death" can be the impetus for becoming a saint.

God was the center of Nick's life and nothing, or no one, could cause him to divert his attention or thinking otherwise. He so impressed all of us who cared for him that we grew to know God in a different kind of way and in doing so we learned what love really means. It is true, "God is love."

In tragedies like the one Nick suffered, people will often ask, "Why does God allow such things to happen?" Every time we ask this question we must remember that God did not cause this to happen. An angry man did. But, with Nick's consent, God took the tragedy and caused much good to come from it.

"A Man" To Remember

So, in caring for Nick, we learned the answer to this question. It is so that we, as human beings, have the opportunity to care for another human being and thereby learn what love really means and the profound power that it has to heal wounds.

In Nick's case he was reduced to being unable to do anything to care for himself. So, without our help, he could not live. But in ministering to Nick, and others like him, we define what it means to be human. We discover the soul in a way we would never know it if we did not perform this service.

While we helped Nick with his life, he lifted ours to a new spiritual level that only this kind of caring can bring—and it is a wonderful place to be. Only love can take you there; otherwise you will not go. Many people came into Nick's life to care for him but did not love enough to reach this level. The ones who paid tribute to him in this book (and many others) did love enough and their spirits are renewed because of it.

Nick lived in hospitals and nursing homes for five years before coming home. It took about seven years to help Nick rehabilitate his life and then the following fifteen years were spent enjoying that wonderful life. There was time to enjoy great meals, attend selected movies, read good books, sit in the sun, swing in a gazebo for hours, relax in the Jacuzzi, go for walks, plan and enjoy wonderful picnics, 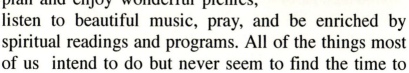 listen to beautiful music, pray, and be enriched by spiritual readings and programs. All of the things most of us intend to do but never seem to find the time to accomplish. The days and weeks and months and years spent this way with Nick were some of the sweetest anyone can imagine.

But during the last few months of Nick's life his health slowly ebbed away and we tried with all of our might to deny it was happening. We did not want to lose this wonderful person who was so much a part of our daily lives.

It is my belief that something happened in his brain during the last four or five months of his life to cause him to slowly lose muscle control in most parts of his body. He finally came to a point where he could no longer stand without help; he could no longer walk in his beloved walking bar; he could not hold up his one good arm; and he needed more help than ever with everything he did.

It takes muscles to breathe and to swallow food and to talk and Nick was having difficulty with all of these activities. I think he knew before we did that life was becoming too difficult to continue living.

Nevertheless, we monitored every function of his body daily and hovered over him to try to make things better—when we could not.

The Sunday before Nick died on Tuesday, he had the most wonderful opportunity of his life. Father Bob from St. Teresa's Church in Woodbury was invited to our home by our son-in-law Tom, who is a Eucharistic Minister in that church, to give Nick the Sacrament of the Anointing of the Sick. Nick's father and I were in attendance along with Mary and Tom and his beloved Nicole and his aide Theresa. Father Bob lovingly anointed Nick and through it all he was totally aware of what was going on.

At last Father Bob told Nick, "When you die Nick, you are going straight into Heaven. All of your sins for your entire life are forgiven and any punishment for them. You will go to the arms of Jesus the moment of your death." Nick's father noticed how he heaved a sigh and visibly relaxed as Father Bob gave him this wonderful blessing. I think Nick's father heaved a sigh and relaxed too.

This was a moment that had to be experienced to fully appreciate the beauty and value of its import. None of us will ever forget it. At times like this you become keenly aware of what the priesthood means and the awesome power that Jesus Christ bestowed on them when they administer sacraments like this one. God bless them all.

The next day Gail hoisted Nick out of bed with his *barrier free lift*. He was bathed, ate very little of his breakfast and then sat in his big overstuffed rocking chair. His feet moved him back and forth as he sat in contemplation for long periods of time. His brother, Joe, and his sister, Debbie, came for a visit with him.

Both Mary and Gail were exceedingly worried about his physical condition as were his father and I. He was losing weight because he wasn't getting much nutrition. He was quieter than ever. All of us laid our heads on our pillows that night but our sleep was disturbed by thoughts of what to do for Nick. Hospice had been called and they were in the first stages of coming to our home to counsel us.

On Tuesday Nick did not want to get out of bed. Mary came early to tend to her brother until Gail arrived. There was an unusual aura of love that started to pervade the atmosphere.

"A Man" To Remember

As was their custom, Mary read the Bible to Nick and he listened and gestured his appreciation. He tried to swallow a few bites of food but was not very successful. I was worried about his medications and called hospice. They arranged to have his seizure medications put in the form of a suppository.

It was strange how, as the morning turned to afternoon, those who loved Nick seemed to stop in to see him. Debbie Vienneau came and so did Nicole. All day long we talked with Carly by phone as she was on vacation. John came home for a short spell. Mary had stayed with Nick and Gail until 11:00 o'clock that morning and then left for work. She came back at 3:00 o'clock in the afternoon because she was so concerned about him. She was startled at the change in his color and demeanor in such a short period of time. I was here all the time and didn't notice it as dramatically as she did.

Through all of this activity the aura of love I had noticed in the morning grew and grew to the point where it was almost visible. For sure it could be felt. I have never experienced anything like it.

Nick's aide Theresa came at 4:00 o'clock for her shift of duty with Nick. She too was shocked at the change in his condition. Theresa had only worked with Nick for a few months but in that short time had come to love this man deeply. She took Mary to one side and told her that there was someone or something that Nick was waiting for before he would let go. Mary told her that she didn't understand the relationship between Nick and his mother. Nick did not want to leave me.

It was true that we had a special relationship from the moment he was born. Nick was an unusual child in that his charming personality was always apparent, even as a baby. He was a very bright child and loved to have me read to him. I thought he could actually read the words. Finally, I discovered he had memorized the story from the pictures as I read to him. Eddie Fisher made a song famous that Nick memorized when he was just a tot. It was *Oh My Papa*. Nick could enchant everyone with his rendition of that song with his little boy voice.

As he grew into an adolescent he learned to judge people quickly and accurately. I always waited for him to get home from school the first day each year. I could tell how the year would go by the way he talked about his teacher.

On one occasion I became so angry with a story he was telling me about an incident in school that I left home immediately to demand that I see his teacher. His sixth grade was a miserable year because of the nun who was teaching his class. Her ravings could be heard by other classes nearby because she was so loud. Larry, Nick's buddy and best friend all through grammar school, brought a tape recorder to school and tried to tape one of her outlandish sessions. She discovered the tape recorder and accused Nick of being in on this stunt because he and Larry were so close. She made Nick stand up in front of the class while she berated him and said she could not punish him the way she did the others because his father was a lawyer.

It was a rule that any visitor had to see the principal before going to a teacher's classroom. When I entered the principal's office, she knew immediately how upset I was and tried to calm me down. I insisted on going to see Nick's teacher but she refused my request and said she would take care of the matter. She must have been afraid of what I would do when I confronted the nun about her behavior.

It is ironic that Larry died just two days before Nick. His wake was in the same funeral home at the same time as Nick's and they were buried in the same cemetery on the same day.

Nick and I talked about everything. I could not help it because he was always so insistent. One day, when he was a young boy, Nick was watching television and came running to me to say he needed an explanation about something. A girl on the TV was having a baby and she was not married. He asked, "How can that be?"

I told him that he needed to have a talk about this with his father and he said, "Why should I, you're here. You tell me." So, I sat him down and we talked about sex and what it means to have a child. It was one of the sweetest talks we ever had. However, it meant his father was going to get out of a bargain we had made. I was to instruct all six girls about sex and he would do the two boys.

Nick was the entertainer in our family. He loved to make us all smile and would do all

"A Man" To Remember

kinds of antics to make us laugh. He was always coming up with skits and jokes to amuse us.

Whenever he did not get the response he was expecting he would say, "You have to be hilarious to get a laugh in this house." He was right. We were a pretty tough audience.

Gifts from Nick would often be very unusual ones. Like the time he caught a fish with his bare hands for his brother on his birthday. And the time he took me to a movie for Mother's Day and detailed for me all the exceptional camera angles. Often a gift would be a book that pertained to a particular problem in the recipient's life or a music album that he thought they should have.

To say my relationship with Nick was exceptional is to put it mildly. I admired this child, this young boy, this man, with every fiber of my being. Perhaps it was because he was so much like his father. Nick returned my love fully.

I was not just his mother, I was a woman and Nick expected and required a level of love, trust, understanding and faithfulness of women that was admirable. He demanded this of me and his sisters and any young women he dated. If you did not meet his standard, you did not have his respect. This trait was very much in evidence after injury as well. It is why four women loved and cared for him so long.

After he came home from the nursing home, this blind, helpless, man never once told me "no" to anything I asked him to do. It was the reason his

"A Man" To Remember

recovery was so remarkable. Nick wanted to live as fully as he could and he instinctively knew that I was the key to his recovery. When others could not get the stubborn Nick to do something, they would call me and I would cajole him into doing it. I kidded with him just like I had always done and he responded with his usual charm and good humor.

In the years after his injury my admiration for Nick heightened into a deep and unfathomable love. I watched this young man come out of coma into a nightmare and he took his situation and made a beautiful dream of it when that seemed impossible to do. He grew into a middle-aged man with grace and dignity under the most difficult circumstances one could imagine.

I think that one of the hardest things I ever had to do was to sit beside Nick's bed and hold his hand while I told him that it was alright for him to go to his other Mother. I described how he had loved her from the time he was a little boy and that she loved him too. I told him how she was the most beautiful woman who had ever been born and that she was waiting for him. "It's okay to go to her, Nick," I told him. Those were the hardest words I have ever had to speak.

Nick and I had a habit of singing Alleluias because it was an easy word for him to say and it always put him in a great mood. That afternoon, with everyone hovering around his bed, I started singing Alleluias to him over and over. It was a bit awkward with everyone listening to me but it was something I felt would mean a lot to Nick and that was all I cared about. The "Alleluias" were sung very softly as we had learned how to do when we made a trip to one of

Father Diorio's healing services in Massachusetts—a long, long time ago.

I just kept singing and singing and I knew Nick was listening and enjoying it. To my astonishment everyone else began to join in and soon the room was filled with Alleluias. As we sang them over and over and over we heard Nick say in a loud voice—one that he had not been able to muster in a long time—"Alleluia." I was pleased and happy as the tears rolled down my cheeks. That "Alleluia" was the last word he spoke.

Hospice came with the dreaded suppository but Nick did not want me to give it to him. I waited. At 5:30 p.m., our pastor, Father John Bevins, came to give Nick a blessing. Once again Nick listened as he assured him of his place in Heaven and read Bible passages to him. As he was leaving he placed a cross in Nick's hand that had been blessed. The cross remained in Nicks hand and was buried with him.

All of us took turns sitting beside Nick's bed to comfort him and read to him and make his stay in bed as pleasant as we could. All day long Nick would try to raise his hand, the gesture he used for God. He could only hold it up for a little while and it would flop back down on the bed. Then he would try again with the same result. But he would not stop. All day long his left hand kept going up and then it would come crashing down because he did not have the muscle strength to hold it up any longer. He rejected any offer to have someone hold his arm up for him.

It was heartbreaking to watch him try to reach for God but one of the most inspirational things I have ever witnessed. He simply would not give up on his connection with God—that raised hand with the fingers that reached heavenward.

I decided to wait in the next room as others had their turn with Nick. Soon Mary went into Nick's bedroom because she wanted some time alone with him and also to relieve Debbie Vienneau who was sitting beside his bed. Just as she got there Nick exhaled—and then, just did not take in another breath. Nick had died.

The life Nick had known on earth was now over as his spirit soared to Heaven. In a split second we were able to behold what it is like when our spirit no longer inhabits our body. It is an awesome realization. The part of Nick we loved so much was no longer encased in that crippled body he had lived with so long. It was free! Free to soar! Now he could see; now he could behold his angels and could embrace, (with both hands), his God he loved so much.

The nurse from hospice was sitting in the living room. She called the funeral director. Mary, Gail, Debbie and I quickly acted to dress Nick as we did not want anyone else touching him. We chose the maroon pants and black shirt that looked so good on him. Gail lovingly covered his neatly pedicured feet with special stockings and then his shoes. Gail was the only one who was ever allowed to cut his toenails.

Mary put the gold cross she had given him around his neck and his onyx ring on his finger. Gail got the Ten Commandments necklace she had given him and put it around his neck too.

Ray Albini from the funeral home came, and was very solicitous of us. When they put Nick on the stretcher to take him out the attendant quickly zipped the bag closed. I interrupted and said, "No, wait," and

"A Man" To Remember

Ray told the attendant to unzip the bag. I had to give Nick one last kiss before he left.

John and Mary and I had talked about his funeral with Nick. None of us wanted him to be embalmed. His body had had enough done to it. However, this meant we would have to have a quick burial. I called Father Bevins to tell him that Nick had died. It had been only two hours since he left our home. We made plans with Father Bevins to have a service at the funeral home with just the family and close friends in attendance and then a Memorial Mass later. Even so, there were about forty people at Nick's burial service. Nick's nephews were his pallbearers.

The service was beautiful and not at all like most wakes. We talked and waited for the priest to come. Peter got up before the assembled group and gave an impromptu talk about his Uncle Nick. Friends met our grown-up children they had not seen in many years. Joan came home from California so that all members of Nick's family were together at last.

At the gravesite the priest said prayers and gave the last blessing of the church to Nick. The flag draping his coffin was folded by men from the Air Force and presented to me. Rifles were discharged and "taps" was played. The atmosphere was very solemn and also serene.

I had arranged for roses to be given to everyone present and we all laid them on Nick's coffin as we slowly left the cemetery to head home for food and conversations about Nick. As sad as it was, it was a glorious day.

A few days later I was looking out the window of Nick's bedroom and noticed a flurry of color. On closer inspection I realized that a rose bush that I had thought dead was blooming with about a dozen small pink roses. I went outside to inspect the garden and found there was also a lily that was in full bloom that I didn't even know was in the garden. The roses bloomed for weeks and I shall protect it carefully through the winter to see if it blooms again next year.

Another morning I was sitting on the back deck having a cup of coffee when I noticed a butterfly flitting around me and going from one part of the deck to the other. It never flew off the deck. Ordinarily I would not have thought anything about that but this butterfly was different in that it was totally black. It stayed on the deck the entire time I was there. The next morning I did the same thing and the black butterfly returned. How could I help but think it had something to do with Nick? One morning John and Mary joined me and they saw the black butterfly too. I was glad that someone other than I had seen it. This happened for about four or five days in a row and then I never saw the black butterfly again.

When our grandson Jason was killed by a drunk driver I experienced another "miracle" of roses. His mother had given me a rose bush that had been planted for years. It never bloomed though the leaves were green and healthy. The summer that Jason died, red roses bloomed all over the bush and lasted for weeks. The next year—no roses. It has not bloomed since.

A week after Nick was buried a Memorial Mass was said at our church for him and a reception afterward in the church hall. So many people who had been influential in Nick's life came and many who were friends of the family. I sat between John and Joan Faulkner (his very special physical therapist who Nick once called a wizard). Dr. Alan Chatt and his wife Gail were present. It was a difficult journey for them to come since he could not drive and Gail Chatt was having problems with her eyes. Dr. Sarfaty was there too.

Nick had chosen the songs and Bible readings he wanted read at his Mass. *How Great Thou Art, On Eagle's Wings, Amazing Grace* and the beautiful *Peace* song were the ones he chose. As the last song played, a trumpet in the choir loft softly played its words:

> *"Peace I leave with you, my friends,*
> *peace the world cannot give.*
> *Peace I leave with you my friends,*
> *so that your joy be ever full."*

"A Man" To Remember

The First Reading was from the Old Testament
Book of Sirach,
Chapter 2, Verses 1-6:

My son, when you come to serve the Lord,
Prepare yourself for trials.
Be sincere of heart and steadfast,
Undisturbed in time of adversity.

Cling to him, forsake him not,
Thus will your future be great.
Accept whatever befalls you,
In crushing misfortune be patient;

For in fire gold is tested,
And worthy men in the crucible of humiliation.
Trust God and he will help you;
Make straight your ways and hope in him.

The Second Reading is from the New Testament
Epistle of Paul to The Romans.
Chapter 5, Verses 1-5:

Now that we have been justified by faith,
We are at peace with God
Through our Lord Jesus Christ.

Through him we have gained access by faith
To the grace in which we now stand,
And we boast of our hope for the glory of God.

But not only that—we even boast of our afflictions!
We know that affliction makes for endurance,
And endurance for tested virtue,
And tested virtue for hope.

And this hope will not leave us disappointed,
Because the love of God
has been poured out in our hearts
through the Holy Spirit
who has been given to us.

"A Man" To Remember

The Gospel Reading he chose from the
New Testament Gospel of Matthew,
Chapter 11, Verses 25-30:

On one occasion Jesus spoke thus;

"Father, Lord of heaven and earth,
to you I offer praise;
for what you have hidden from the learned
and the clever
you have revealed to the merest children.

Father, it is true
You have graciously willed it so

Everything has been given over to me
by my Father.
No one knows the Son but the Father,
And no one knows the Father but the Son—
And anyone to whom the Son
wishes to reveal him.

"Come to me, all you who are weary
and find life burdensome, and
I will refresh you.

Take my yoke upon your shoulders
And learn from me.
For I am gentle and humble of heart.
Your souls will find rest.

For my yoke is easy
And my burden light."

These songs and readings are so like Nick and tell a story about him that no other words can express.

"A Man" To Remember

Nicole and Johnny, his namesakes, did two of the Bible readings and Amy, Mary's daughter, did another. Zachary, Gail's son, led the Prayers of the Faithful and Gail, Spencer and Brandon brought up the gifts to the altar. Nick's father gave a speech about him and his sainthood and then I gave a eulogy for Nick. How I ever managed to have the courage and the strength to give this eulogy I will never know.

I repeated the poem "A Man" by Emily Dickinson that is the opening of this book. And then I said:

Acknowledged a man? Oh yes! One of the bravest, most courageous, stout-hearted men I have ever known. How could he endure life reduced to its lowest level physically? One that none of us would ever say we want to live. Because he *LOVED LIFE* and he *LOVED GOD*.

He said this every day after he was so brutally injured. After the Nick we knew lost the life he had known in a pool of blood on a YMCA floor, he became like "Phoenix Rising" to a new life that would inspire all who came close to him. How did he do it? He simply loved God and God helped him take the spirit inside of him to a state of perfection few people on this earth will ever get to know.

The world loves physical beauty but cares little about spiritual perfection. Nick gave us the opportunity to see the physical side of his life unable to do anything alone except breathe, and then watch a soul mature, grow, and become a thing of indescribable beauty.

He was counselor to all of us who talked about our daily problems with him. He listened patiently and then gave his advice. *LOVE GOD*. This advice seemed so trite in the beginning. But then he would repeat it to us over and over. *LOVE GOD*. After a time we were able to absorb this sage advice and realize that all of the problems of the entire world could be solved with his two-word admonition. *LOVE GOD*.

If ever a soul, separated from a body at death, flew to heaven, then Nick's has been transported on the swift wings of the angels he used to tell us he sees.

"Look in my eyes," he would say. "I see God and angels working on me."

Nick, God and His angels don't have to work on you any more. You are a shining star in God's heaven if ever there was one.

God bless you, Nick, in your new life of perfection as you still inspire us to *LOVE GOD*.

There is a saying I'm sure Nick would wish to leave with you. It goes like this:

> The golden sun comes up each day
> Although the blind man never sees it
> And so to those who won't believe
> Unless they see—I say believe it!

Printed in the United States
23986LVS00002B/34-69